H. J. EYSENCK

KNOW YOUR OWN

I. Q.

PENGUIN BOOKS

PENGUIN BOOKS

Published by the Penguin Group
Penguin Books Ltd, 27 Wrights Lane, London W8 5TZ, England
Penguin Books USA Inc., 375 Hudson Street, New York, New York 10014, USA
Penguin Books Australia Ltd, Ringwood, Victoria, Australia
Penguin Books Canada Ltd, 10 Alcorn Avenue, Toronto, Ontario, Canada M4V 3B2
Penguin Books (NZ) Ltd, 182–190 Wairau Road, Auckland 10, New Zealand

Penguin Books Ltd, Registered Offices: Harmondsworth, Middlesex, England

First published in Pelican Books 1962
Reprinted in Penguin Books 1990
9 10 8

Printed in England by Clays Ltd, St Ives plc
Set in Monotype Times

CONTENTS

INTRODUCTION
INTELLIGENCE QUOTIENTS AND THE
MEASUREMENT OF INTELLIGENCE

'KNOW yourself!' was one of the slogans which the ancient Greeks bequeathed to us, and although such knowledge may not always be as beneficial and useful as ancient Greeks and modern psychoanalysts believe, nevertheless there is no doubt that most people have an intense interest in their own personality, temperament, intelligence, traits, abilities, complexes, and so forth. I have often lectured on the nature and measurement of intelligence to lay audiences, and I have nearly always noted their disappointment when I have told them that there was no easy and direct way in which they could measure their own I.Q. The present book is designed to remedy this state of affairs, and to enable anyone with sufficient intelligence to follow the instructions to obtain a reasonably accurate measure of his or her intelligence quotient. In making this possible, the book may contribute in a very small way to the realization of the precept quoted at the beginning of this paragraph.

Before embarking on this enterprise, however, the reader might be well advised to look through the remainder of this chapter which explains briefly and, I hope, clearly, just what an I.Q. is, how it is determined, what its implications are, and to what limitations and criticisms its use is subject. A little knowledge, as we have been told so often, is a dangerous thing, and possession of this book will no more transform the reader into an expert psychologist than the purchase of a thermometer will transform him into a physician. Nevertheless, it may be of interest or importance to know whether one has a fever or not, and clearly the possession of the thermometer can help in producing an answer to this question even though the owner has received no medical training.

In discussing the measurement of intelligence I think it is necessary first of all to squash one widely held misconception. It is often believed that intelligence tests are developed and constructed according to a rationale deriving from some sound scientific theory; it is also widely believed, however, that however 'scientific' the measurement of intelligence may be, its practical value is very poor, particularly because of certain inherent difficulties in going from the ivory tower to the market place, and the alleged inapplicability of psychological science to practical problems of applied life. In actual fact the position is exactly reversed. Intelligence tests are not based on any very sound scientific principles, and there is not a great deal of agreement among experts regarding the nature of intelligence. Arguments about this subject were very popular in the 1920s and 1930s, but they have pretty well ceased now because it is realized that they were largely verbal and did not permit of any reasonable solution. On the other hand, intelligence tests, right from the beginning, have been outstandingly successful in their practical application; we shall consider shortly what is meant by saying that an intelligence test is 'successful', but the evidence on this point is so overwhelming that no one familiar with even a small part of it is likely to regard this statement as an exaggeration.

In part, these two apparently contradictory facts – intelligence testing has no firm scientific basis, and intelligence testing is very successful in its application – are in reality complementary. Because the intelligence tests, originally constructed in the early years of this century, did such a good job when applied to various practical problems, psychologists interested in the subject tended to become technologists, eager to exploit and improve these tools, rather than scientists eager to carry out the requisite fundamental research, most of which still remains to be done. Society, of course, always interested in the immediate application of technological advances and uninterested in pure research, must bear its share of the responsibility for this unfortunate state of affairs. It has always been far easier to obtain research money for technological investigations destined to improve in some slight way an existing instrument, or to apply it to some new group, than to carry out the highly abstract, complex, and not immediately useful work of laying a firm scientific foundation for the measurement of intelligence.

The reader may be surprised that useful measurement can be undertaken in the absence of a sound theoretical basis. In answer we may perhaps go back to the analogy of the thermometer used previously. The measurement of temperature starts out with a rough and ready psychological observation, to wit, that our sense organs perceive different degrees of temperature ranging from very cold through average to very hot. Subjective estimates of this quality are clearly not very accurate. The reader may like to try the following experiment. Prepare three bowls of water. One of these is filled with water as hot as can be borne without extreme discomfort; one is filled with water near the freezing point; and the middle bowl is filled with lukewarm water. If the reader will now immerse his left hand in the hot water for one minute, and his right hand in the cold water, and then transfer both simultaneously to the middle bowl, he will find that to his right hand the lukewarm water appears unbearably hot, while to his left hand it seems intensely cold. Thus clearly the same temperature may appear as hot or cold according to an immediately preceding experience. Or the reader may like to try another experiment. Let him invite an American friend during the winter into what he fondly believes to be his adequately heated home. He will soon find that what to him is warm is excessively cold to his American friend, used to living in rooms heated to temperatures ten to fifteen degrees higher than is usual in this country.

We thus start with a very subjective, but nevertheless real, entity, which can be measured very, very roughly in subjective terms. Indeed such measurement made in terms of the reactions of living beings, rather than in terms of physics, can be surprisingly accurate, as witness Dolbear's law. This was enunciated by the physicist, Dolbear, in 1897, working with snowy tree crickets, and it runs like this: 'Count the number of chirps this animal produces in fifteen seconds and add forty; the sum is the temperature obtaining at the time in degrees Fahrenheit.'

However, snowy tree crickets are rare and difficult to get hold of, and they cannot easily be integrated into the general system of physical laws on which our system of measurement is based. Consequently, it was widely recognized when the thermometer was invented that a very significant advance had in fact been made, and people ceased to measure temperature in terms of their own reactions of hot and cold, and instead used the contraction and expansion of a variety of substances. Now the important point to remember is this. There is no perfect relationship between thermometer readings and subjective individual judgements. If we regard the latter as a criterion, and the former as the test whose validity we wish to investigate, we would have to conclude that the test left much to be desired. In the case of the thermometer, of course, we realize full well that the lack of perfect relationship is due to faults in the criterion, i.e. to irregularities and errors in our subjective judgements, and not to faults in the test itself; much the same may be true when we compare the results of a test of intelligence with our subjective notions of a person's intelligence. Failure to agree may be due to faults in the test, but they are perhaps more likely to be due to errors in our subjective estimates.

Another point may be worth looking at. At the time the thermometer was invented there was little in the way of scientific theory regarding the nature of heat or its measurement. The measurement of temperature was not derived from an advanced theoretical analysis of heat; rather the modern theory of heat was very much based on results obtained through the use of the thermometer and other measuring instruments. This fact should by borne in mind by many people who take a rather purist view of scientific advance and will have nothing to do with tests of intelligence until we have a perfect theory of its nature. This is to misperceive the nature of scientific advance in any subject; the theory tends to be the end product and the crowning glory of a long series of investigations starting with new discoveries and new measuring instruments. The invention of the intelligence test will undoubtedly in due course lead to a better understanding of mental processes, and indeed in many ways it has already done so. What one might rightfully complain of would be that too little time has in fact been devoted by psychologists to the scientific exploitation of this new discovery, as opposed to its commercial and applied use.

The first beginnings of the testing movement are less than a century old. Psychology is the child of two rather dissimilar parents: philosophy, which provided many of its early problems, and physiology, which suggested many of its early methods. Philosophers have always been interested in the cognitive powers of the mind, i.e. those concerned with intellectual pursuits, thinking, and the perception of the outer world, and it seemed to the early psychologists that possibly some such physiological notions as the relative speed of nervous impulses in the central nervous system might be relevant to differences in intellectual ability. A number of approaches were tried, including the measurement of the speed of response of the patellar tendon reflex, i.e. the speed with which the foot shoots up when you tap the knee-cap with a rubber hammer. The upshot of all this work was largely negative; either neurological differences of the type investigated do not discriminate highly intelligent students from mental defectives, or the methods used were not refined enough to reveal such differences. The same was found to be true when attempts were made to weigh and dissect the brains of very able and very dull people; some slight differences were found but these were too indefinite to suggest that this was a fruitful approach. Finally the French psychologist, Binet, came up with what was not only the right answer, but one which would now appear an obvious one, to wit, that mental abilities and functions should be measured by means of mental tests clearly involving these abilities and functions. In 1904 the Ministry of Public Instruction in Paris appointed a commission to study procedures for the education of mentally subnormal children attending Paris schools, and it was in response to this practical demand that Binet prepared his first scale. He constructed a series of thirty problems or tests which were meant to call for judgement, comprehension, and reasoning. The problems were of such a nature that they could be understood and solved without benefit of special school learning. Thus the child might be presented with a card bearing a circle with a gap in it;

he would be given a pencil and told: 'This is a garden in which you have lost your ball; this gap represents the entrance. Use your pencil to show me how you would search for your ball.' Any systematic search, i.e. in ever-decreasing circles, or going up and down along parallel paths, is counted as a correct solution, whilst a vague wandering about is counted as incorrect.

The problems varied widely in difficulty, and Binet graded them from the easiest to the most difficult by noting the percentage of right answers given by various groups of children. This approach finally lead him to the concept of *mental age*, by means of which he grouped at the three-year-old level all the tests normally passed by three-year-olds, at the four-year-old level all the tests passed by normal four-year-olds, and so on. Having done this, he was now able to apportion a mental age to any child who did the test, by noting the highest difficulty level at which he was successful. Thus a child who succeeded with the eight-year-old tests but failed with the nine-year-old tests was said to have a mental age of eight, regardless of his chronological age. Allowances can, of course, be made for additional tests passed, so that a child who passed all those at the eight-year-old level and half of those at the nine-year-old level would have a mental age of eight and a half. Early workers expressed a child's intelligence or dullness in terms of the difference between his chronological age and his mental age. Thus a child of ten with a mental age of eight would be two years retarded, while a child of six with a mental age of nine would be three years advanced. This is not a good way of expressing mental superiority or mental inferiority, for two related reasons. In a child of two, to be two years advanced is an extremely rare and very noticeable achievement; less than one child in 50,000 would achieve such a distinction. To be two years advanced at the age of thirteen or fourteen is barely noticeable and does not mean very much. Thus clearly a more uniform yardstick is needed. Furthermore, if you measure children repeatedly you find that the number of years of advancement or retardation increases as they get older. The child who is two years advanced at the age of two would be something like eight years advanced at the age of eight. Thus what remains constant is the *ratio* of mental age over chronological age, rather than the *difference*, and it is this ratio (usually multiplied by 100 to get rid of the decimal point) which is referred to as the intelligence quotient. Let us consider two children, both with a mental age of eight. The first has a chronological age of six, and his I.Q. would therefore be 133; the other has a chronological age of twelve and his I.Q. would therefore be 67. The I.Q. has achieved immediate popularity, and in spite of its many imperfections it has remained probably one of the most widely known psychological concepts among teachers, psychiatrists, social workers, and others connected in some way with psychology.

What do the two different I.Q.s mean in social terms, and how frequent are people of I.Q. 140 say, or I.Q. 80? Let us take the latter point first. On a typical modern test of intelligence you would find about 50 per cent of the population between I.Q.s of 90 and 110, 25 per cent above and 25 per cent below. (The 100 mark is, of course, by definition, the average of the population.) Above this large central group you have about 14·5 per cent with I.Q.s of 110 to 120, 7 per cent with I.Q.s between 120 and 130, 3 per cent with I.Q.s between 130 and 140, and only ½ per cent above 140. Quite roughly you would expect grammar-school places to go to children with I.Q.s above 115 or thereabouts, and you would expect university students to average about 125 I.Q. To get a first-class degree, or some equivalent distinction, a student would probably have to have an I.Q. of 135 or 140 at least.

When we turn to the below-average level we find a complementary picture, with 14·5 per cent having I.Q.s between 80 and 90, 7 per cent having I.Q.s between 70 and 80, and the rest having I.Q.s below this level. Actually this very symmetrical picture giving the same percentages above and below the mean is somewhat idealized; there is a small number of specific metabolic and other disorders affecting intelligence adversely and increasing the number of individuals with very low I.Q.s; however, we have not paid any attention to this small group in our descriptive scheme.

People with I.Q.s below 70 are sometimes classified in the

textbooks as feeble-minded, and there is an even more precise distinction within this group, dividing it up into morons, with I.Q.s between 50 and 70, imbeciles with I.Q.s between 25 and 50, and idiots below 25. The moron, it is said, can learn useful tasks, and adjust under supervision. The imbecile has to live in an institution, but can care for simple personal wants and avoid simple dangers, whilst the idiot cannot even do this. In actual fact, however, certification for feeble-mindedness is made on a much more comprehensive criterion than a simple I.Q. test, and in any case it has little to do with intelligence. When inmates of mental-defective institutions are tested, some are found to have I.Q.s as high as 125, and while this may be due in many cases to errors in the original testing, which in the past used to be carried out entirely by medical officers having little training in the administration of intelligence tests, and little knowledge in interpreting the results, nevertheless the point remains that the concept of mental defect in its legal aspect is only perfunctorily related to intelligence.

We would expect intelligence tests to show differences in mental ability between people in different types of jobs, related to the intellectual requirements of these jobs. Many such studies have been made, and the table below shows some of these results in which I.Q.s of groups of people in eight different social strata are given. These are listed under the heading, 'parents'. (There is a similar column for 'children'. This does not mean that these particular children had these particular parents, but simply that the children had parents in the same social group.)

I.Q.s of groups in eight different social strata

PROFESSIONAL GROUP	I.Q.	
	Parents	*Children*
1. Higher professional and administrative	153	120
2. Lower professional; technical and executive	132	115
3. Highly skilled; clerical	117	110
4. Skilled	109	105

PROFESSIONAL GROUP		I.Q.	
		Parents	Children
5.	Semi-skilled	98	97
6.	Unskilled	87	92
7.	Casual	82	89
8.	Institutional	57	67

These figures are taken from a table published by Sir Cyril Burt.

We are here concerned with the figures given for parents; the fact that those for children are quite different will be discussed later. It will be seen that there is a regular descent from the higher professional and administrative group, with a mean I.Q. of 153, to the unskilled and casual workers, with I.Q.s in the low 80s. These, of course, are average figures for all groups; there is considerable overlap usually between members of one group and those of another. The brightest dustman would undoubtedly score much higher than the dullest lawyer; the brightest tramp better than the dullest physician; the brightest navvy higher than the dullest captain. The total relationship between intelligence and social status is quite marked but very far from perfect; if you try to predict a person's intelligence from knowing his job you would be right more frequently than if you were guessing by chance, but you would still be wrong so frequently that the exercise would not be worth while.

So much for the distribution of intelligence and its 'meaning' in terms of occupation and social status.

We must now turn to some of the difficulties to which the concept of I.Q. gives rise. First of all there is the problem of *constancy*. We may obviously use the I.Q. in two different ways. We may say: here are two children, which of them has a higher I.Q. and is, therefore, better suited to do this difficult job than the other? In this way we would be regarding the I.Q. as a measure of present ability, regardless of its future implications. We may, however, use it in quite a different way by saying: which of these two children has the higher I.Q.; we will give him a grammar-school education while the other one will receive his education in a secondary modern school. So here we are using the I.Q. as a semi-permanent characteristic of the child, assuming that because he is brighter now he will remain brighter for the rest of his life. If we make this second assumption, which is clearly implied in such procedures as the 11+ examination, then we must be able to show that the I.Q. remains relatively constant from year to year, i.e. that the child who has an I.Q. of 120 when he goes up for his 11+ does not turn out to have one of 80 when he leaves school.

This problem of determining the constancy of the I.Q. is a very complex one, but ultimately it boils down to a simple comparison of the I.Q. achieved by a child at one age, and the I.Q. achieved by the same child at a later age. This comparison is affected by several factors. In the first place it depends on the age of the child on the occasion of the first testing. I.Q.s obtained at very young ages are practically worthless, and except in cases of severe mental defect I.Q.s obtained before the age of six are of very little use. The relationship between one set of variables and another is usually expressed in terms of the correlation coefficient which attains the value of one when in perfect agreement, and a value of zero when there is nothing but chance agreement. When the I.Q.s obtained from children of four years or thereabouts are compared with their I.Q.s when they are grown up it is usually found that their correlations are very low, usually not far from zero, so that prediction is impossible. Six, therefore, is perhaps the lowest age at which I.Q. tests are to be taken at all seriously – and even at that age they should not be taken *very* seriously!

The second variable that comes into our consideration is that the agreement between the original and the terminal testing declines as the number of years increases, or, expressed in different terms, the correlation between original and terminal tests gets less the longer the time that elapses between the two occasions. There appears to be a reasonable lawful relationship here. If the original and terminal tests are very close together, i.e. separated by a week or less, then the correlation will be in the neighbourhood of ·95. For every year that passes it drops by ·04 points until the age of sixteen or so.

This leads us to the third consideration, and that is the terminal age. By the time an individual has reached maturity his I.Q. has stabilized to a very considerable extent and is not likely to change very much, provided that the individual's central nervous system is not attacked by physical illness. Thus the correlation between initial and terminal tests, if both are given after the age of twenty or so, will tend to be around the ·8 mark regardless of the length of time intervening.

In terms of this discussion it will be fairly obvious that many protagonists in the 11+ debate are defending positions which are not supported by facts. Adherents of present-day procedures are wrong in suggesting that the I.Q. of the eleven-year-old is firmly fixed; there are very definite changes which are likely to take place, and in some children at least these changes can be quite considerable. Those who condemn the 11+ on the grounds that children's intelligence has not sufficiently settled down by the age of eleven to make prediction possible are also wrong, because prediction, while not perfect, is certainly possible to a degree and with an accuracy which is not often realized by the uninitiated. As so often in matters of fact both sides are trying to argue the case in terms of their preconceptions rather than in terms of established data.

It may be worth while at this point to illustrate the remarks I made at the beginning of this chapter regarding the technological use of intelligence tests in the absence of fundamental scientific inquiry. Tests are made and validated in terms of the first type of use I mentioned a paragraph or two ago, i.e. in terms of comparing little Johnny here and now with little Jimmy here and now. There is no obvious reason why the particular test problems which are adequate for this purpose should also be those best suited for predicting the relative intelligence of little Johnny and little Jimmy ten years hence. Indeed one or two small-scale inquiries have followed groups of children up until their adult I.Q.s were available, and have compared the predictive excellence of each item in the test with its usefulness in defining the present intellectual status of the child. The outcome was that there was little relationship between the two concepts, i.e. an item which is a good measure of a child's intelligence *at the present moment* may or may not be a good measure of his *future ability*. If we want to use our intelligence tests as measures of future as well as present ability, a use clearly implied in the procedure of the 11+, then surely a great deal of research should be done into this problem, and entirely new sets of tests evolved which would give even better predictive accuracy than the ones in current use. As far as I know no such research is being done, and no effort is being made to improve existing tests along these lines. Until work on the subject is begun we are not likely to obtain any further knowledge about the reasons why some children increase and some decrease in their I.Q., how these changes can be predicted, and whether there is anything we can do to influence them in any way by accelerating the upswings and cutting out the downswings.

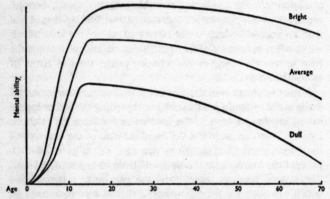

Fig. 1. The growth and decline of mental ability with age, in bright, dull, and average groups of people.

Granted that the I.Q. is *reasonably* constant under certain strictly specified conditions, we next come to a notable difficulty in determining I.Q.s for older children and for adults. The growth and decline of mental ability with age has been investigated by many psychologists, and the results seem to be rather as indicated in the diagram in Figure 1. There is a fairly rapid growth from birth to twelve years or so which then slows down, reaches its peak around fifteen, remains reasonably level for a while and then declines. This is the average picture, but the average can be very misleading. In individuals of low intelligence, i.e. with I.Q.s of 80 or below, growth ceases earlier, decline sets in earlier, and is itself more precipitous, than would be true for the large medium group with I.Q.s between 90 and 110. Conversely, those with high I.Q.s, i.e. with I.Q.s of 120 or above, have more prolonged growth and a slower decline. Now it will be clear that the growth of intelligence is reasonably linear only between the ages of about six to twelve, and it follows that we cannot properly calculate an I.Q. beyond the age of twelve or fifteen at the most. This will become clear to the reader if he will imagine a perfectly average individual who has a chronological age of fifteen and a mental age of fifteen, thus giving him an I.Q. of 100. As Figure 1 shows, his mental age will not increase but will remain pretty steady. His chronological age, however, will go on increasing until at the chronological age of thirty, with a mental age of fifteen, he has an I.Q. of 50! At the age of sixty with his mental age actually decreasing while his chronological age is still increasing he would have an I.Q. of about 20. Clearly this is nonsense, and the I.Q. defined as a ratio of mental and chronological age is not applicable after the age of twelve or fifteen.

What we do in order to get out of this difficulty is a rather simple statistical transformation trick. We still give to our subjects a kind of intelligence test, and we still count the number of correct solutions each subject has achieved. We next find out the average number of correct answers; this, being the average or mean response for the group, is identified as an I.Q. of 100, which, again by definition, is the average or mean I.Q. of the group. In a similar manner we find out the limits between which 50 per cent of all the scores lie, and identify these limits with the I.Q.s of 90 and 110. In this way we can continue to match the distribution of point scores with known distribution of I.Q.s until we can express each point score as an individual I.Q. score. Giving an adult an I.Q., therefore, is a kind of make-believe operation; what we are saying to him in effect is that if the concept of the I.Q. could be applied at his age *then* this is the I.Q. he would have got. There are, of course, better statistical methods of indicating a person's relative ability, but the concept of the I.Q. has become so widely known and its implications are so well understood by non-psychologists that more would perhaps have been lost by giving it up than by retaining it in this purely statistical connotation.

We must now turn to the question of the validity of the I.Q. as a measure of intelligence. Here we come up right from the beginning against the difficulty that no satisfactory criterion does in fact exist. Agreement among laymen about the nature of intelligence, or acceptable evidence for its existence, is even lower than it is among experts; indeed one might argue that if there were in existence a really satisfactory criterion, then intelligence tests would probably be superfluous altogether! However, on a rough and ready basis we might all be prepared to agree that people of high intelligence will, other things being equal, succeed better at intellectual tasks, i.e. tasks involving learning of interconnected new facts and principles, the application of such facts and principles to new situations, the invention or discovery of relations between existing facts, and other similar tasks. In part at least, though certainly not completely so, schools and universities attempt to introduce pupils and students to areas of knowledge requiring the use of such abilities, and the success of the student is in part measured by examinations. It is, of course, realized that many other factors determine examination success, in addition to intellectual ability, and we would not expect any perfect relationship between success at school and university and I.Q.; nevertheless if no relationship were found at all, then we would be exceedingly suspicious of the value of our tests.

The results of very large numbers of carefully planned investigations support the conclusion that I.Q. tests, properly constructed, administered, and evaluated, show considerable agreement with the success of the child at school, or the adolescent at university. Students who obtain a first-class degree have usually scored some ten I.Q. points higher on the occasion of their first entering university than did students obtaining lower-class degrees; successful students have usually scored some fifteen points higher than students who failed to obtain a degree at all. The close relationship found between I.Q. and success at university is somewhat surprising in view of the fact that the total *range of ability* of all students is very much restricted by the fact that hardly anyone with an I.Q. of less than 115 is likely to be admitted to university because of the fairly tough preselection policy adopted by universities. This means that differences in I.Q. between university students are relatively slight, thus making successful prediction more difficult. The fact that under these conditions quite high correlations are in fact obtained is a good indicator of the value of I.Q. tests as measures of ability. This success should be compared with the almost unrelieved record of failure which has attended traditional methods of selection by means of interview procedures. It has been found time and again that there is practically no relationship between predictions of academic success made by experienced interviewers unaided by I.Q. tests, and academic success. Thus obviously I.Q. tests do succeed in measuring something vital in this field which is not apparent even to experienced interviewers and experts who have spent many years in perfecting their subjective judgements.

It is often contended that the opinion of the class teacher of a child's intelligence is of more value than examination results, but when correlations are run between ratings made by class teachers and I.Q. tests there tends to be a fairly close relationship. It is interesting in all these cases to study the failures of agreement, i.e. those cases where intelligence test and class teacher, or intelligence test and examination results, disagree. When this is done it is usually found that the disagreement is due to one or other of the following factors:

(1) The class teacher's opinion of the child's intelligence is too much dependent on the child's special ability or interest in the particular subject taught by the class teacher. This can often be shown by comparing ratings made by several teachers of the same set of children; little Johnny will tend to be rated high by his English teacher because he likes the subject and is fairly good at

it, but he is rated low in intelligence by the Maths teacher because he loathes and abominates mathematics, and is no good at figures. Conversely Jimmy, who has the same I.Q. as Johnny, is rated high by the Maths teacher and low by the English teacher because he likes playing around with figures but is no good with words. The intelligence test is not influenced by such extraneous and irrelevant considerations, and has often been found to correlate more highly with the ratings of the same group of children made by different teachers, *than do these ratings among themselves*. The highest correlations are usually obtained by comparing the I.Q. results with ratings made by a group of teachers, where such individual likes and dislikes cancel out.

(2) A child or a student may fail an examination not because of lack of intelligence but because of lack of persistence. Clearly a certain amount of application is required before the subject matter can be mastered, and there is no reason to assume that the bright child will necessarily apply himself more strongly and more willingly than does a rather duller child. Fortunately it is possible to measure objectively such character traits as persistence (as I have discussed in *Sense and Nonsense in Psychology*), and the results demonstrate quite clearly that this is indeed an important factor additional to, and independent of, intelligence. Intelligence tests are often criticized for not paying attention to such important matters as character and personality, and persistence is often mentioned as one of the qualities that determines success. Nevertheless the objection is not well taken. You do not object to the thermometer because it only tells you the temperature of the patient, and not his height and weight; it is realized that a scientific measuring instrument is useful and valuable to the degree to which it measures one quality only. The I.Q. test measures intelligence, and to the degree to which it measures other things, such as persistence, it would be considered to fail in its primary objective. If we wish to know about a person's persistence, his proneness to anxiety, or any other personality trait, then we should not expect this information to be provided by a test of intelligence. If indeed an I.Q. were determined simultaneously by intelligence, persistence, and anxiety, then the fact that little

Johnny had an I.Q. of 90 could be due to the fact that he was very dull but persistent and little prone to anxiety, or it could be due to the fact that he was very bright but anxious and lacking in persistence. It might be due in fact to any number of interactions of these elements, so the information would be very nearly useless in the absence of any knowledge of little Johnny's standing in these three qualities separately. If we wish to know a person's intelligence, persistence, and anxiety, then we require three measures, not one, and to criticize a measure of intelligence because it tells us nothing about non-intellectual qualities is not a reasonable criticism.

(3) A third cause of disagreement between I.Q. measures and external criteria may be related to motivation. If we can take a horse to the water, so we can send a child to school, but as we cannot make the horse drink so we cannot make the child learn unless he is in fact motivated. It is sometimes argued by critics of I.Q. tests that Winston Churchill, to take but one example, was very bad at school, and very slow in acquiring academic knowledge; it is argued from this that he would have done badly on I.Q. tests, and that his consequent demonstration of high ability disproves the value of tests. Apart from the obvious absurdity of begging the question, i.e. assuming that he would have done badly on tests when no test was in fact administered, this argument breaks down because it assumes that he was motivated to acquire school learning. His autobiography clearly contradicts this assumption, and indeed it is often found, particularly with very able children, that teaching of school subjects in a manner appropriate to the average I.Q. of their class makes them rebel to such an extent that they prefer to go their own way, read what interests them, and pay no attention to what they are taught. Under those conditions the very bright child may do poorly in examinations, only to come into his own later in life when ability and motivation come together in pursuit of some worth while goal. This, of course, does not always happen, and there are many extremely able people who fail in achievement because of defects in motivation.

These are the main causes of disagreement in test and performance or test and rating, but, of course, there are innumerable reasons why a person may not live up to his promise. From a case file of students of very high I.Q. who failed to obtain a degree, I have taken at random the following cases. T.S., I.Q. 152, repeatedly failed his medical course. His father died just as he was entering university, and he had to support himself, his mother, and a younger sister by night work which left him too little time and energy to pursue his very exacting studies. D.R., with an I.Q. of 146, was expelled from his college in spite of superior performance because he was found to steal money from his fellow students. S.B., with an I.Q. of 161, failed to complete his course of study, running away instead with his professor's wife. The list could be extended almost indefinitely.

People with low I.Q.s do not on the whole do well in academic and intellectual pursuits; this is as near to an unalterable law as psychology has yet come. The reason, of course, is that intelligence is a necessary prerequisite for success, and that no amount of persistence or any other quality can make up for lack of ability. The converse, however, is not true. Intelligence is a necessary but not a sufficient cause of success, and consequently students of high intelligence may or may not succeed, depending on circumstances, personal qualities, degree of motivation, and many other non-intellectual factors. Some of these, like persistence, can be measured, others cannot, either because we have not advanced sufficiently to measure them accurately, or because in principle it is unlikely that they could ever be measured. There are, therefore, definite limitations to the kind of prediction that can be made by I.Q. tests, but nevertheless once these are understood it becomes easier to appreciate the very definite contribution which can be made by these tests.

Are teachers' ratings, success at school, and success at college the only criteria which can be applied to intelligence tests? The answer to this question is definitely in the negative, although the further away we go from academic pursuits the more easily are doubts raised about the actual relevance of intelligence to the pursuits in question. Perhaps the most widespread use of intelligence and other ability tests has been in the armed forces where such tests have been used for selection purposes. This work began in the United States during the First World War, and led directly from the use of individually administered tests of the Binet type to group tests, such as the ones presented in this book, which can be given to large groups at a time. The purpose of these tests was primarily to help in the selection of officers, and to weed out mental defectives. Their success was so obvious, even to the conservative military mind, that their use has spread throughout the western world, and nowadays these tests are used for selection of a very varied group of different specialists in the Army. To give the reader an idea of the kind of results obtained I am reproducing as Figures 2 and 3 the results of two very large-scale studies, involving large numbers of people, dealing with the selection of officer candidates on the one hand, and of pilots on the other. Both studies were carried out in the United States during the Second World War, and in the case of the pilot selection, ability tests other than I.Q. tests were used in addition to make up a whole battery given to prospective candidates.

The diagrams largely speak for themselves. Of all those men with a score of 140 or over on the A.G.C.T. (Army General Classification Test) over 90 per cent were successful in receiving a commission; of those with a score under 110 less than 50 per cent received a commission. In the case of the pilots, of those in what is referred to as 'pilot stanine 9', i.e. with the highest scores on the test battery, only 4 per cent were eliminated in primary pilot training; of those in 'pilot stanine 1', i.e. scoring lowest on the battery, 77 per cent were eliminated. It will be noted also that there is a regular progression in each case from one extreme to the other, in such a way that as test performance increases so probability of failure decreases.

The reader may be impressed with the demonstration of such a definite relationship, but may wonder why the relationship is not even closer than shown in these figures. The answer to this question lies largely in defects associated with the criterion. To obtain very close correlations between a test and a criterion, the criterion, as well as the test, has to be well-nigh perfect. In the case of the two studies referred to above, the criterion was

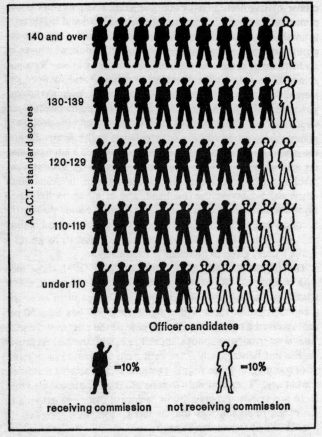

Fig. 2. (Quoted by permission of E. G. Boring from *Psychology for the Armed Services*.)

success in officer training course in the one case, and success in primary flight training in the other. There is ample evidence to show that these criteria are by no means perfect, but are attended by considerable error. Thus a candidate might be accepted as an officer by one committee, but rejected by another. Similarly a pilot might succeed with one set of teachers but fail with another. A detailed discussion of the evidence would be too technical to be useful here, but an impartial examination of the facts suggests that failure of the relationship to be very close indeed is much more likely to be due to faults in the criterion than to faults in the tests themselves. Thus it would seem in the military field as well, and in spite of the fact that both officers and pilots obviously need many qualities other than high mental ability, nevertheless intelligence tests are of considerable practical use as selection devices.

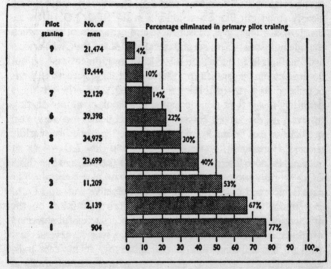

Pilot stanine	No. of men	Percentage eliminated in primary pilot training
9	21,474	4%
8	19,444	10%
7	32,129	14%
6	39,398	22%
5	34,975	30%
4	23,699	40%
3	11,209	53%
2	2,139	67%
1	904	77%

Fig. 3. (Quoted by permission of J. C. Flanagan from *Science*, 1947.)

As a last example we may perhaps take success in everyday life. Here again it will be obvious that this is determined by many qualities other than intelligence, such as persistence, luck, connections, impudence, aggressiveness, and the like. But, nevertheless, we would again be doubtful of the value of intelligence tests if they showed no relationship at all with worldly success. Some of the evidence has already been presented in the table on pages 14–15, where there is shown a clear trend for I.Q. to be related to position on the social sphere. Other studies have correlated I.Q. with money earnings, showing that there also a distinct relationship could be demonstrated. There are, of course, definite limitations to this argument, as well as to the data on which it is based. There are some groups of high intelligence, notably academic teachers, university lecturers, and also school teachers, whose high intelligence on tests is not rewarded by society in a manner commensurate with their contribution. If one were to draw a graph relating I.Q. to money earnings, then those groups would clearly stand out like a sore thumb in the 'high I.Q. – low-to-medium earnings' group. But these and other exceptions, which include industrial scientists and certain grades of the Civil Service, are intelligible in terms of historical development and do not contradict our generalization that by and large success in life is correlated to a reasonable extent with I.Q. This relationship is definitely lower than that obtaining at school, or at universities, or even in the armed forces, and consequently no very firm predictions can be made from I.Q. to the likelihood of worldly success. Here again the negative prediction (low I.Q. – lack of success) is more likely to be accurate than the positive one (high I.Q. – worldly success), although this is by no means certain. The case is recorded of at least one mental defective with an I.Q. of just under 70 who was released from an institution on the application of his wife and who became a successful salesman owning a large house in town, a villa at the seaside, several cars, with all his children away at the university. In his case luck, extraverted temperament, and other temperamental qualities probably played an unduly large part in leading him to success, but his case (which is not unique) does demonstrate the precariousness of any predictions which could be made from I.Q. to likely income level.

We have considered so far some of the objections which can be made against I.Q. tests and have found them lacking. We must now consider some other objections which are perhaps better founded, and which restrict in important ways the usefulness of I.Q.s unless care is taken to overcome these difficulties. The first objection which is quite frequently made relates to the effects of practice and coaching. Obviously it would be unfair to compare the I.Q.s of two children, one of whom had never seen an intelligence test before while the other had received intensive coaching in tests of that type, unless it could be demonstrated that this coaching had no effect whatsoever. The position is rather complicated, but the facts seem to be as follows. Most children obtain higher I.Q.s on the second or third occasion that they do an intelligence test, even though the test may be quite a different one each time. This rise in I.Q. may be from between five to seven or eight points, and is most likely due to the acquisition of test sophistication, the knowledge of procedure, reduction in the anxiety which is natural when people are presented with something new, and simple practice in solving the kinds of problems presented in tests of this type. There is little if any gain after the administration of three intelligence tests. Coaching may add a little to the simple act of doing the test but this is doubtful and in any case may differ with the type of coaching received; it is quite possible that unskilful coaching may lower rather than raise the increase in I.Q. points to be expected from simply doing a series of tests. The criticism that practice and coaching affect I.Q.s must therefore be admitted, but fortunately the difficulties raised by this fact can easily be circumvented by testing children, students, or candidates not just once but several times. 11+ examinations in particular should never be given to children who have not been thoroughly acclimatized to the taking of intelligence tests, and when this precaution is observed little difficulty is likely to be encountered in this connection.

The second objection relates to the effects of motivation and anxiety. May not a poorly motivated child, or one who is terribly anxious about the outcome, fail to do himself justice? There is a large literature on the effects of motivation and anxiety on children, and the indication appears to be that a low degree of motivation is not particularly harmful in doing intelligence tests unless it is so low as to make the candidate give up altogether.

This is rare and almost certainly pathological, and such a test would not, of course, be counted in any case. High levels of anxiety may indeed have a deleterious effect on children, and this would present a serious argument against the use of tests if it had not been found that this anxiety can be decreased in several ways. Much depends on the way in which the test is introduced, and whether it was given by someone known to the child or a stranger. Most important of all is repetition. Anxiety is highest on the first occasion that a new test is introduced, but quickly adaptation sets in, and after three occasions there are very few individuals who would still show levels of anxiety high enough to interfere with their performance. Here again then it is clear that repetition of testing, and getting the child used to doing the tests, holds the key to successful measurement. Indeed, this recommendation has many other arguments in its favour. A single testing may be spoiled for many different reasons. The child may have a headache, or be below par for some other reason. He may be worried or upset by something that has happened to him or to his family. He may have a tummy ache, or his pencils may break; he may have gone to sleep late. There are a thousand and one things, none of which would have a very profound effect on the score, but which if they accumulate could produce quite a marked discrepancy from the child's actual I.Q. If the child is tested repeatedly, however, it is unlikely that these causes would occur each time the test was given and discrepant tests could be excluded from consideration. It is obvious that the average of several tests is more reliable than the score from one test, and where decisions can be extremely important, as in the case of the 11+, a single test score should never be trusted.

This point is also relevant to the next objection frequently made, namely the present I.Q. of the child may not be a good predictor of his I.Q. several years hence. We have already discussed this point in some detail, and have found that while not very relevant to intelligence testing with adults, it does present difficulties in the case of children. The evidence unfortunately is not very broadly based or very conclusive, but it does seem that repetition of I.Q. tests year after year, both before and after the fateful 11+ examination, would give important additional information for a decision of grading or regrading, as well as being useful in alleviating anxiety about the other points previously discussed.

The discussion so far will make it clear that from the point of view of the intelligence tester it is very undesirable to have mixed groups to deal with, i.e. groups some among whom have had previous experience of intelligence tests, while others have not. Ideally, therefore, he would prefer a population where either no one had had any experience with tests, or where everybody had gone through two or three tests of one kind or another. The former state of affairs clearly is unattainable. All children about the age of twelve have had experience with tests, and many adults too have been tested at one time or another, in the armed forces or in connection with some form of vocational selection. Under the circumstances, therefore, the ideal to be aimed at would be that everyone should have had some experience with the types of problems which occur in intelligence tests, and it is from this point of view that I think the appearance of such programmes as 'Pencil and Paper' and 'Pit Your Wits' on television ought to be welcome, where groups amounting to 14,000,000 at a time have become painlessly acquainted with intelligence-test problems and methods of solving them. In a similar way I should imagine that the publication of a book such as this one would be welcome to psychologists seriously concerned with this problem, because it will undoubtedly increase the number of people acquainted with modern intelligence tests. In the not too distant future therefore the ideal will perhaps be realized where everyone in the population has reached a sufficient standard of test sophistication to make all further coaching or practice useless and non-productive.

We must now turn to another objection to the I.Q. which strikes much nearer home than those considered so far. This objection is made more frequently by psychologists than by laymen, and there is no doubt that it is soundly based. The argument runs something like this. The measurement of an I.Q. assumes that we are concerned with one general mental ability called intelligence which determines to a greater or lesser degree our success in a great variety of intellectual tasks. This assumption may only be justified to a limited degree, and it may be that our performance on different tasks is determined not only by one general ability, but in addition by a number of rather more specialized abilities. If this were so then one might regard the I.Q. merely as a kind of average drawn through the different levels of these more specialized abilities, and it would thus partake of all the disadvantages as well as all the advantages known to be possessed by an average.

There are several directions in which we can look for these more circumscribed abilities. The main directions are (a) in the differential content of tests, and (b) in the differential psychological functions involved. Exactly the same type of problem can be presented in an intelligence test in a verbal, numerical, or perceptual-spatial manner, and a person's success may depend on the way in which the problem is presented. Consider the three problems given below:

(1) Black is to white as high is to: (1) low, (2) green, (3) up, (4) far.

(2) 14 is to 7 as 30 is to: (1) 15, (2) 13, (3) 20, (4) 11.

(3) ↑ is to ↓ as → is to: (1) ←, (2) ↑ , (3) ↓ , (4) →.

This surmise has in fact been shown to be correct; the material, whether verbal, spatial, or numerical, determines a person's reactions to a considerable extent, and we are therefore justified up to a point in measuring separately a person's verbal intelligence, his numerical intelligence, his spatial ability, and so on.

Similarly there are differences with respect to mental function which cut across those of material. We may ask our subjects to discover relations and educe correlates, as in the examples given above. We may ask them to compare a variety of different words, or shapes, or numbers, and note similarities and differences. We may ask them to learn by heart, then reproduce from memory, verbal, or numerical, or visuo-spatial items. These are only some of the numerous ways in which we can subdivide both materials and functions, but it can be seen that by only taking three of each we have already nine different types of tests, each differing from the others in at least one important point.

Instead of giving a person a general I.Q. therefore we might be better advised to give him separate tests for each of these combinations and assess his pattern of abilities with respect to his standing in all of these categories. This, of course, is a tall order; there are something like 140 different categories of this kind which would have to be tested, so that at the rate of one hour per test, and a forty-hour week per subject, a reasonably adequate coverage of a person's mental ability will take something in the nature of a whole month of full-time testing! From the practical point of view this of course is not feasible although time periods of this length are not at all unusual in physics when, say, the efficiency of a new engine is being determined, or the fatigue-ability of a metal, where indeed tests may go on for years under standard conditions.

The I.Q. may be regarded as an average which gives a rough idea of the general level of performance on a sample of all these different types of tests; it will differ from test to test according to the actual sample of functions and material selected. Thus some I.Q. tests rely entirely on verbal material, others are entirely non-verbal and many employ only numerical material. Similarly the functions tested, and the form of testing adopted, differ from one test to another, and it follows from all this that different I.Q. tests will not agree very closely in their assessment of the individual's I.Q. The agreement between different well-established tests is usually reasonably close, but it is nevertheless far from perfect, and differences of ten points of I.Q. from one test to another are by no means rare. It follows from what has been said that the best estimates of an individual's I.Q. are likely to be given by tests which use different forms of problems and use also different materials for testing the subject's ability; it is for this reason that the problems in the eight series of tests given in this book have been put together in just this way.

For most practical purposes, such as for vocational guidance or industrial selection, it must be recognized that the I.Q. is probably very much less useful than the more precise measure of the more specific type of ability. If we have to advise little Jimmy and little Johnny, who have now grown up and want to enter university, as to what subjects they would be best suited for, it will not help us much to know that little Johnny has an I.Q. of 135 and little Jimmy one of 128. It will, however, help us considerably to know that on a test of *verbal ability* Jimmy has an I.Q. of 150, Johnny one of 115, while conversely on tests of *numerical* and *visuo-spatial* ability the positions are reversed. Clearly decisions as to whether a study of modern languages or physics is indicated can be made much more easily on the basis of such information than on the basis of a generalized I.Q. This is becoming much more widely realized now than it used to be even ten years ago, but it would still be true to say that tests of specific abilities are not used as widely as they might be. Much of this failure to use these more advanced and powerful methods of testing lies in the conservatism of teachers and others who were brought up on the traditional I.Q. test, and in part the reason lies in the fact that the development of such measuring devices is expensive and requires considerable research spread over many years. Society has not shown itself particularly concerned with the achievement of the improvement on ordinary I.Q. tests held out by modern discoveries, and the failure to support the necessary research has led to the position where few well-standardized tests, suitable for the purpose, are available in this country.

The question is often raised whether intelligence is innate or acquired; this is often referred to as the nature-nurture controversy. Before closing this account of I.Q. tests a few words may perhaps be said about this thorny problem. To begin with, then, it is clear that children tend to resemble their parents with regards to their I.Q.; indeed, until the child is six years of age or thereabouts a better prediction of his future I.Q. is obtained by measuring that of his parents than by measuring his own! However, this fact does not help us very much, as this similarity could clearly be due either to hereditary or environmental factors; the child could resemble his parents because he inherited the genes making for intelligent behaviour, or he could resemble them because he grew up in an environment largely reflecting their intelligence. Actually our main information regarding inheritance of intelligence comes rather from the fact that while children largely do resemble their parents, there are systematic deviations which can only be accounted for in terms of hereditary causes. The phenomenon I have in mind is usually called *regression*, and it was first observed in relation to height, which is known to be very much an inherited characteristic, at least in countries with an adequate food supply. It was found that the children of very tall parents are taller than the average, but not as tall as their parents; similarly, for small parents, their children are smaller than the average, but taller than their parents. On both sides children appear to *regress* to the average, and it is quite simple to account for this fact in terms of the Mendelian theory of heredity. Now exactly the same phenomenon has been observed in relation to intelligence, and if the reader will turn back to the table on pages 14 and 15, which gives the I.Q.s of groups of parents in various social strata, and of children whose parents come from the same social strata, he will see the degree of regression involved, which is almost identical with that found in studies of height. Our main evidence for the importance of heredity therefore comes not from the similarities observed between parents and children but from the discovery of systematic differences between them which find an easy explanation in hereditary terms but which are very difficult to account for along environmental lines.

The second type of proof frequently advanced relates to the study of identical and fraternal twins. Identical twins completely share their heredity while fraternal twins are no more alike than ordinary siblings, i.e. share heredity only to the extent of about 50 per cent. It will be clear that if environment has a strong effect, then identical twins should be no more alike than should fraternal twins, whereas if heredity is a stronger force, then identical twins should be much more alike than fraternal twins. Many studies have dealt with twins brought up together, and the universal findings have been that identical twins are very much more alike. Rather small-scale studies in the United States, and a recent rather more extensive study in Great Britain, have shown that when you take twins, separated early in life and brought up under different conditions, there nevertheless remains a definite tendency for the identical ones to be more alike than the fraternal ones. This method of investigation also strongly favours the hereditary rather than the environmentalistic point of view.

As a third proof you may perhaps look at breeding studies done with animals. Here a test of ability suitable for the animal in question is constructed, and a group of animals is tested. High scorers are then interbred to produce a bright strain and low-scoring animals are interbred to produce a dull strain. The animals in each successive generation are tested, and the brightest and dullest ones respectively are picked out and interbred again. After a dozen or so generations it is found that there is practically no overlap in performance between the bright and the dull strains, all the bright offspring doing better on the test than any of the dull. The weight we would place on this evidence depends of course on whether we view intelligence as a biological characteristic which is not necessarily confined to humans but can also be assessed, although at a rather lower level, in other mammals. It is perhaps in conjunction with the other proofs already advanced that this one assumes particular importance.

A fourth proof is in a sense the obverse of the one in which identical twins were used. In the twin experiments we keep heredity identical and let the environment vary; clearly we can attempt instead to keep the environment constant and let heredity vary. This is done by studying orphanage children sent there shortly after birth. The whole life of these children is spent in an environment which is practically identical for all the children; if environment determines intelligence, then all the children should have very similar I.Q.s to each other. Only heredity could produce differences in I.Q. between the children. When this experiment was done, it was found that intelligence in orphanage children showed practically the same degree of variability as intelligence in normal children subject to great differences in environmental conditions; here again therefore heredity appears as the prime factor in the determination of individual differences in intelligence.

Many other types of tests and types of experimental design have been tried, but those mentioned above are the most conclusive ones, and they are not contradicted by any other evidence. They indicate quite clearly the importance of heredity, and it is possible to define a rough and ready numerical estimate for the relative contribution of heredity and environment in Western countries at the present time. It appears that about 80 per cent of all the factors contributing to individual differences of intelligence are hereditary, 20 per cent environmental; in other words, heredity is four times as important as environment.

It should be noted that these figures are rough averages only, and that they only apply to the Western world at the present time. They have no absolute value, since they depend entirely on the social and educational practices in a given country. Where there is universal free education for all children, and possibly universal free access to university education as well, then obviously hereditary factors are most free to manifest themselves. In countries where there is education only for a privileged few, the potential intelligence of the others may be repressed to a considerable degree. We cannot therefore extrapolate the '80 per cent – 20 per cent' figure to apply to this country one hundred years ago, or to Iran at the present time, to take but two examples, nor can we extrapolate them into the future; it is quite possible that in fifty years' time the relative contribution of heredity to the results of intelligence tests will be even higher than it is now, provided the trend towards greater equality in education continues.

One last qualification to what I have said so far is necessary. I mentioned that the figures are only averages; that means that it would not be true to say that for any given person environment contributed 20 per cent and heredity 80 per cent to his intellectual endowment. There are some children and adults, grossly deprived of educational and other facilities during their lives, where the importance of environment would be very much higher, perhaps as high as 70 or 80 per cent. There will also be other children where the balance is tilted in the other direction. To say anything in a specific case would require a much closer and more detailed study than the simple application of a general average.

So much then for this brief account of intelligence, its nature and its measurement. The field is a highly technical one and it is almost impossible to present it in common-sense terms and in very brief compass without occasionally appearing dogmatic. Nevertheless, most of the facts are fairly clear and I do not believe that many professional psychologists would have serious faults to find with anything said so far. It may even be that in twenty years' time we will know a little more about the actual nature of intelligence than we do at the present; until then we shall have to remain content with our ability to measure it with a certain degree of accuracy, and with such data as can be collected by means of intelligence tests.

HOW TO MEASURE YOUR OWN I.Q.

WE must now turn to the consideration of the tests printed in this book, and the possible uses which may be made of them. There are eight tests, consisting of forty problems each; each test is a complete entity in itself, and can be used and scored without reference to the other seven. Each test consists of a varied series of different types of problems with the easiest at the beginning and the most difficult at the end, although it should not be assumed that the difficulty levels in between are very carefully graded. Each test should be timed, preferably by someone other than the person doing the test, and for each test a time-limit of thirty minutes is set. Thus thirty minutes after commencing on the first problem the test should be completed, and no further work done on it; the score of course is the number of correctly answered problems obtained by this time. The answers are given at the end of the book, together with explanations as to why the given answer is the correct one. The score on the test in points should then be looked up in the tables on pages 191-2, where the corresponding I.Q. can be read off. The other seven tests should be treated in exactly the same way so that the reader will end up with eight separate assessments of his I.Q. which can then be averaged to give a more accurate assessment than any single test score would give. (The reader is not advised to do more than one test on any particular day, but to spread tests over several days.) Alternatively the tests in the book may be used to test eight different people, or to give two tests to each of four people, and so forth.

To make the test a reasonably valid one certain definite precautions should be observed. The reader is of course free to do what he likes with the book, but if any of these precautions are neglected, then the result of the test has no claim whatsoever to represent even an approximation to an I.Q. measurement. In the first place then the time assessment must be exact; even a 'few seconds' added at the end may make a good deal of difference. It is best to have a stopwatch handy for the purpose but an ordinary watch with a second hand will do provided somebody reliable is available to do the timing.

In the second place no help of any kind must be given to the person doing the test by anybody else; indeed it is much preferable if nobody else watches the test being done. The administration of an intelligence test may seem a fairly routine procedure, particularly when the test is a group one, but even so most psychologists have occasionally experienced some rather shocking departures from the methods laid down. Thus teachers, who often administer such tests, occasionally give way to the ingrained habit of correcting errors and point an accusing finger at little Johnny's answer to a problem saying: 'That is not right!', in addition to prompting or in other ways interfering. Other people have a distracting influence and should be kept away from the room where the test is being done.

The reader should come to the tests quite fresh and should not vaguely leaf through the actual test material before beginning to work on the problems. Failure to obey this instruction gives him an advantage over those people on whom the test was standardized which will of course vary with the length of time spent on looking at the problems, but in any case such practice would considerably decrease the meaningfulness of the test result.

The reader should not score any test, or look at the explanations given with the solutions, until he has finished *all* the tests he himself is going to do. Checking on the solutions, and reading the reasons given, are equivalent to coaching and will therefore increase his scores on subsequent tests beyond what they would otherwise have been. If the reader desires to do all eight tests, he should not score the first test until after he has finished the eighth. This is a rather difficult injunction to obey, as many people are very keen on knowing the results of their efforts; where curiosity cannot be held in check the reader may get somebody else who has already done the tests, or is in any case not going to do them, to score the tests for him, and translate the result into an I.Q. This degree of knowledge is permissible and will not help in getting higher scores on later occasions.

Once the reader has determined his I.Q. on the basis of one or more of the tests in the book, he should realize that there is a certain amount of spurious accuracy involved in any single figure purporting to give a measure of his intelligence. To say that a test reveals a person's I.Q. to be 128 is unduly optimistic; what the result really means is something like this: 'This chap is quite bright, with an average level of performance probably lying between 120 and 135. He may in addition be outstandingly good or bad in certain more specialized fields such as verbal intelligence, or numerical intelligence, or with respect to originality or memory; this we cannot tell from the test result.' If a similar I.Q. comes up on each of the eight tests in this book, then the average is probably quite a good approximation to the true I.Q.

If there is a good deal of variability then one would regard the average as not being terribly trustworthy. It should be noted, however, that this variability is not necessarily a fault of the test. There is ample evidence that some individuals have a general tendency to be more variable in their performance on any kind of test, and this is a personality characteristic which may come out on tests of this type as well.

What use can be made of an I.Q. thus determined? I should say the reader will be best advised to regard it strictly as helping him to 'know himself' in the spirit of the opening paragraph of this book. *He should not base any serious decisions on the result*, such as whether or not he is qualified to go to university, take a particular kind of job, or to undertake a particular type of work. If he needs advice on any of these points then he should go to a properly qualified organization, such as the National Institute of Industrial Psychology, or the Psychological Department of his local university, where he will be given expert advice and guidance, and be tested on a professional basis. As I have pointed out before, there is no reason why one should not take one's own temperature, but there is every reason in the world why one should not diagnose one's own illnesses on the basis of the thermometer reading in the absence of a medical training. I do not believe that there is any harm in determining one's own I.Q. in a rough and ready manner, but there is every reason in the world why the interpretation of the results, or their application for practical purposes, should be left to someone with suitable qualifications. This is all the more true when it is realized that there are far more errors that can be made in determining one's own I.Q. than in determining one's temperature, and while I have warned against some obvious errors it is impossible to anticipate and rule out all the things a person might do which would invalidate the measurement of his I.Q. In brief, the tests of this book should be used for amusement only, and should not be taken very seriously. If any decisions are to be made involving the true knowledge of a person's intelligence, then the tests contained in this book are emphatically not sufficient and should be supplemented by tests selected and applied by a properly qualified psychologist.

INSTRUCTIONS

EACH test contains forty items. You have a limited time (see p.39) to work out the answers, so work as quickly as possible. Don't linger too long over any item; you may be on the wrong track altogether, and might do better with the next one. On the other hand don't give up *too* easily; most of the problems can be worked out with a bit of patience. Just use your common sense in judging when to leave an item unsolved. And remember that on the whole items tend to get more difficult later in the test. Everybody should be able to do *some* items correctly, but nobody should be able to do *all* the items correctly in the time allowed.

Your answer in each case will consist of a single number, letter, or word. You may have to choose from various alternatives given to you, or you may have to think up the right answer. Indicate your answer clearly in the appropriate space. If you can't figure out the answer, don't guess; but if you have an idea but aren't quite sure if it is in fact the correct one, put it in. There are no 'trick' questions, but you should always consider a variety of ways of approaching the problem. Be sure you understand what is required of you before you start on a problem; you waste time if you go straight ahead without bothering to find out just what the problem is.

For a few of the problems alternative answers which genuinely meet every requirement of the problem may occasionally be hit upon by the reader. Should this occur, the reader may count his answer as correct.

NOTE: Dots indicate the number of letters in a missing word; thus (. . . .) shows that the missing word you are required to find has four letters.

TEST ONE

1. Insert the missing number.

2   5   8   11   __

2. Underline the odd-man-out.

house   igloo   bungalow   office   hut

3. Find the missing numbers.

7   10   9   12   11   __   __

4. Underline the odd-man-out.

herring   whale   shark   barracuda   cod

5. Underline which of these is not a make of car.

ROFD
RAGNUDAV
TEYLENB
METOC
TAIF

6. Insert the word missing from the brackets.

fee (tip) end
dance (....) sphere

7. Insert the word that completes the first word and starts the second. (Clue: Leave.)

IN (...) TER

8. Which of the six numbered figures fits into the vacant square? (Insert the number in the square.)

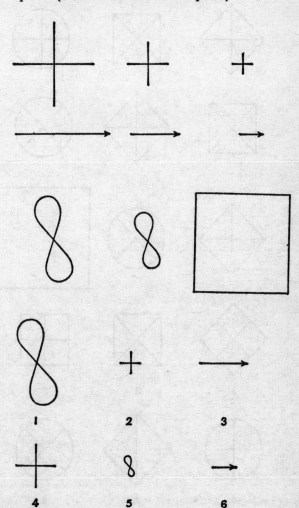

9. Which of the six numbered figures fits into the vacant square? (Insert the number in the square.)

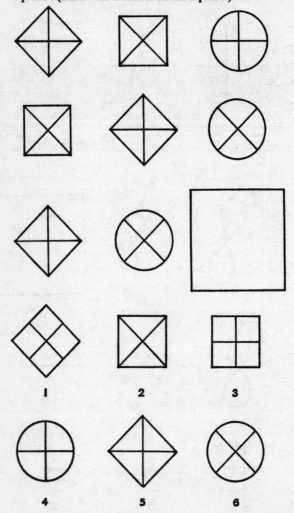

10. Insert the missing number.

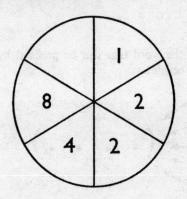

11. Underline the odd-man-out.

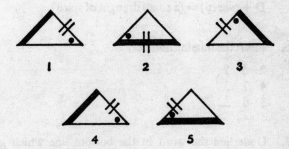

12. Insert the missing numbers.

16	15	17	14	
32	33	31	34	

13. Insert the missing letter.

E   H   L   O   S   _

14. Insert the word that can be prefixed by any of the letters on the left.

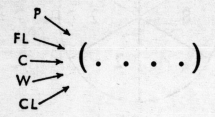

15. Find the words in brackets.

D + (sheep) = (a small draught of spirit)

16. Insert the missing number.

2   5   7
4   7   5
3   6   _

17. Underline the word in the bottom line which goes with the three at the top.

BELT   BLOOD   GUARD
tide   water   time   bird   fear   ape

18. Which of the six numbered figures on the opposite page fits into the vacant square? (Insert the number in the square.)

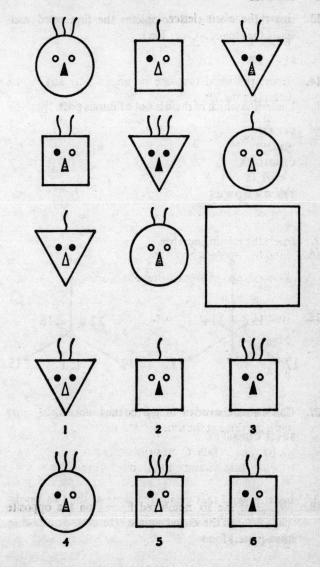

19. Insert the word that completes the first word and starts the second. (Clue: Tie.)

s(...)T

20. Underline which of these is not a famous poet.

STEAK
YORNB
CREHUCA
RANIBAS
THROWDOWRS

21. Insert the missing number.

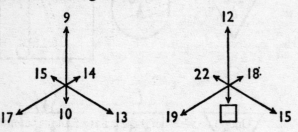

22. Complete the word missing from the brackets.

SE (SUCCESS) CU
NA (G . . L . . T) LA

23. Insert a word that means the same as the two words outside the brackets.

larva (. . . .) food

24.   Underline the odd-man-out.

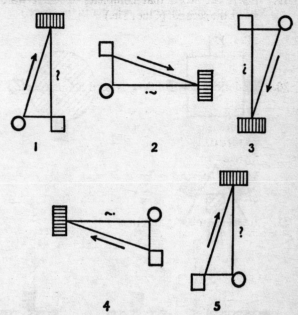

25.   Underline which of these is not a famous composer.

ZOTRAM
SATSURS
REVID
MALESO

26.   Insert the missing letter.

K N H
P T L
I N ?

27. Which of the five numbered figures fits into the vacant space? (Insert the number in the space.)

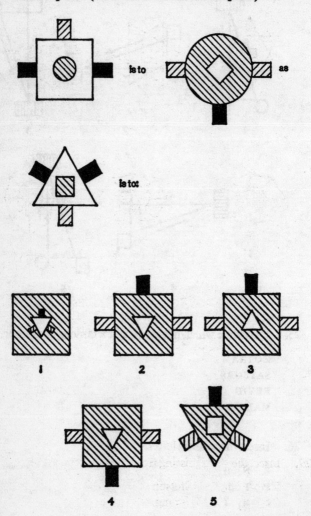

28. Which of the five numbered figures fits into the vacant space? (Insert the number in the space.)

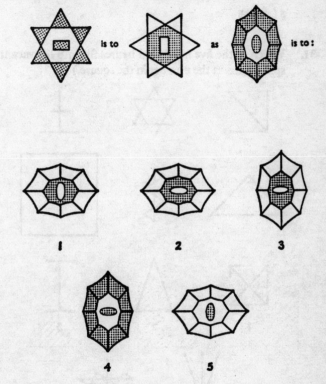

is to ——— as ——— is to:

1

2

3

4

5

29. Insert the word missing from the brackets.

Simpleton (Test) Stetson
Quarry (....) Winning

30. Insert the word that completes the first word and starts the second. (Clue: Spin.)

S (. . .) E

31. Which of the five numbered figures fits into the vacant space? (Insert the number in the square.)

1

2

3

4

5

32. Which of the six numbered figures on the opposite page fits into the vacant square? (Insert the number in the square.)

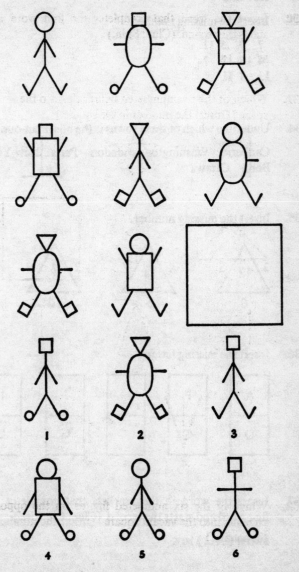

33. Insert the missing number.

    7 9 5 11
    4 15 12 7
    13 8 11 __

34. Underline which of these towns is the odd-man-out.

    Canberra Washington London Paris New York
    Bonn Ottawa

35. Insert the missing number.

36. Insert the missing letters.

A	F		J	I
D	C		G	L

37. Insert the word in the brackets that completes the
    first word and starts the second. (Clue: Chastise.)

    BROW (....) NIK

38. Insert the missing number.

8 10 14 18 ___ 34 50 66

39. Insert the next letter in the series.

A D A E A G A I A M A ___

40. Insert the missing number.

2 7 24 77 ___

TEST TWO

1. Insert the missing number.

8   12   16   20   —

2. Which of the six numbered groups fits into the vacant square? (Insert the number in the square.)

3. Underline the odd-man-out.

lion   fox   giraffe   herring   dog

4. Insert the two missing numbers.

6   9   18   21   42   45   __   __

5. Underline the odd-man-out.

Jupiter   Apollo   Mars   Neptune   Mercury

6. Underline which of these towns is not in Europe.

SHANTE
WOOCSM
LINAM
GATHWONNIS
GAIWN

7. Insert the word missing from the brackets.

chocolate (sweet) darling
hit (....) puff

8. Insert the word that completes the first word and starts the second. (Clue: Animal.)

c (...) x

9. Which of the numbered figures fits into the vacant square? (Insert the number in the square.)

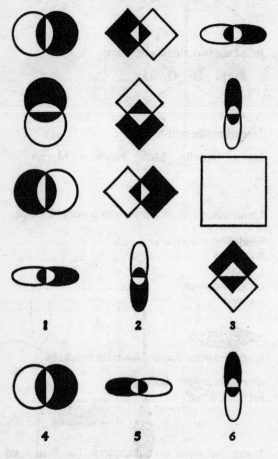

10. Insert the missing letter.

A   D   H   M   S   __

11. Insert the missing number.

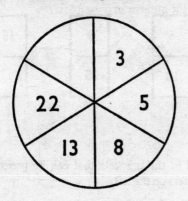

12. Underline the odd-man-out.

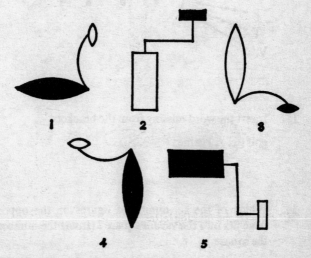

13. Insert the missing number.

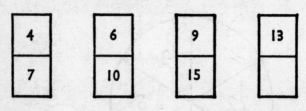

14. Insert the word in the brackets that can be prefixed by any of the letters on the left.

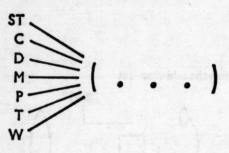

15. Insert the word missing from the brackets.

golf (....) game

16. Which of the six numbered figures on the opposite page fits into the vacant square? (Insert the number in the square.)

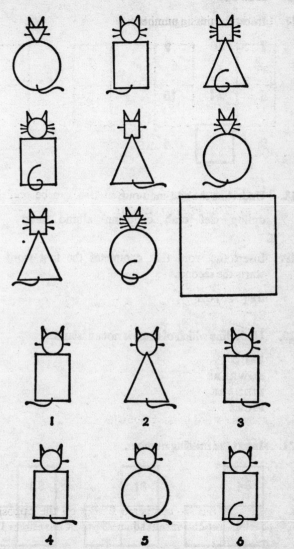

17. Insert the missing number.

7   16   9

5   21   16

9   [ ]   4

18. Underline the odd-man-out.

dollop   clef   crab   condemn   albino   sink

19. Insert the word that completes the first word and starts the second.

DE (...) CH

20. Underline which of these is not an island.

BAUC
POWRARS
LIDNARE
PICRA

21. Insert the missing number.

84	
14	12

81	
18	9

88	
	11

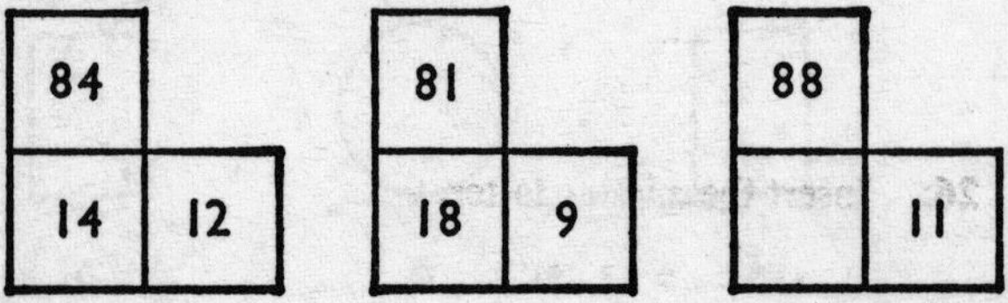

22. Underline the odd-man-out.

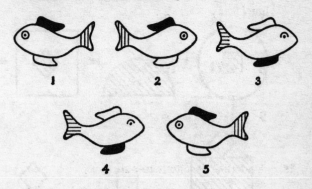

1   2   3

4   5

23. Insert the word missing from the brackets.

54 (hide) 98
53 (. . . .) 16

24. Insert the word that means the same as the two words outside the brackets.

crow (. . . .) swindle

25. Complete the following.

SCOTLAND 27186453   LOTS 7293   LOAN 8367
AND ____

26. Insert the missing letter.

N Q L S J U __

27. Which of the five numbered figures completes the top line?

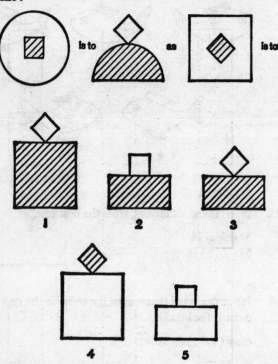

28. Insert the word missing from the brackets.

BQ (CRAM) BN
RK (....) JQ

29. Insert the word that completes the first word and starts the second.

B (...) OW

30. Which of the six numbered figures fits into the vacant square? (Insert the number in the square.)

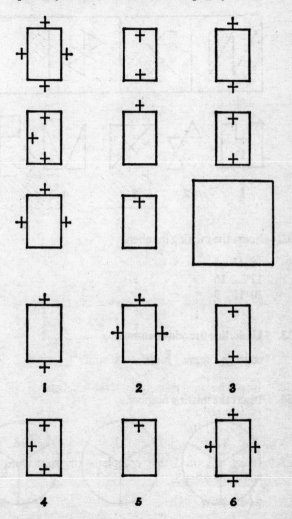

31. Which of the five numbered figures fits into the vacant space? (Insert the number in the square.)

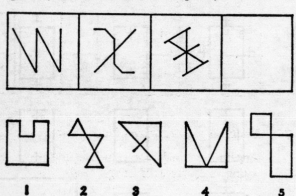

32. Insert the missing number.

```
 8 17  5
12 __ 16
10 11  9
```

33. Underline the odd-man-out.

courage   leave   measles   steamer

34. Insert the missing number.

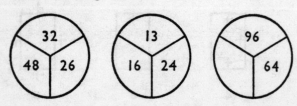

35. Insert the number and letter which are on the next domino in this series.

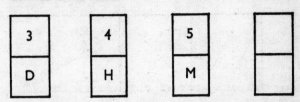

36. Underline the word which completes the sentence.

Appetite is to food as concupiscence is to:
eating sex force gluttony drink

37. Insert the word in brackets that means the same as the two words outside the brackets.

card (. . .) champion

38. Underline the word that completes the sentence.

Palimpsest is to palindrome as erase is to:
repeat reverse retire relive reduce resell

39. Insert the missing letter.

B E — Q Z

40. Insert the number which completes the series.

7 9 40 74 1526

TEST THREE

1.   Insert the missing number.

25   20   15   10   __

2.   Underline the odd-man-out.

chariot   car   bus   waggon   sleigh

3.   Insert the missing number.

3   7   16   35   __

4.   Underline the odd-man-out.

ant   spider   bee   moth   midge

5.   Underline which of these animals whose names are hidden in the jumbled letters below is the smallest.

NOBIS
NETIKT
WROTHAG
USEOM
IRGAFFE

6.   Insert a word which means the same as the two words outside the brackets.

disc (. . . . . .) achievement

7.   Which of the six numbered figures on the opposite page fits into the vacant space? (Insert the number in the square.)

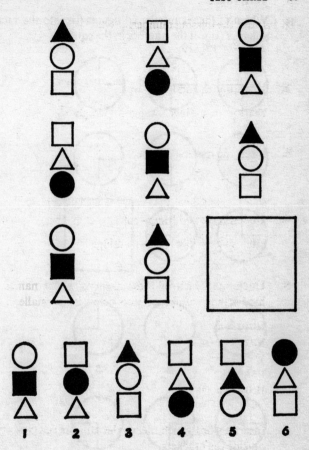

1   2   3   4   5   6

8. Insert the word that completes the first word and starts the second.

SP (. . .) EAR

9. Which of the six numbered figures fits into the vacant square? (Insert the number in the square.)

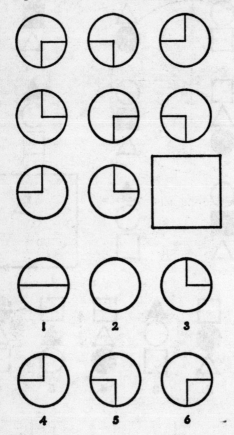

10. Insert the missing letter.

M N O L R I V __

11. Insert the missing number.

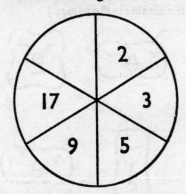

12. Underline the odd-man-out.

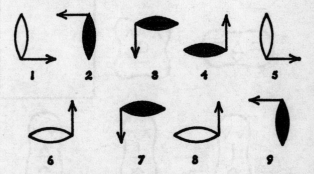

13. Insert the missing numbers.

2	4		11	16
3	7		21	31

14. Which of the six numbered figures fits into the vacant square? (Insert the number in the square.)

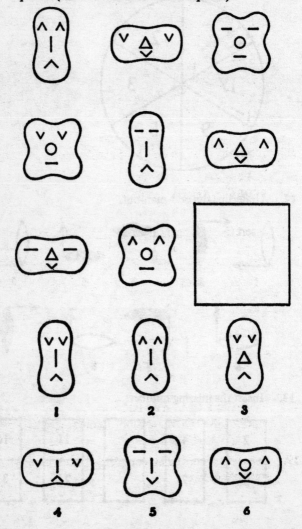

15. Insert the word in the brackets that can be prefixed by any of the letters on the left.

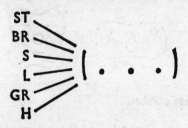

ST
BR
S
L
GR
H
(. . .)

16. Insert the word missing from the brackets.

PAPER (WEIGHT) LIFTER
SHOE (....) BILL

17. Insert the missing number.

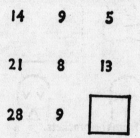

14   9   5

21   8   13

28   9   ☐

18. Underline the odd-man-out.
opulent detergent station hiding ability police

19. Insert the word that completes the first word and starts the second.

KER (.....) TAIN

20.   Underline which of these is not a boy's name.

TEBORR
TEENBICD
LAWMILI
SEVUN

21.   Insert the missing number.

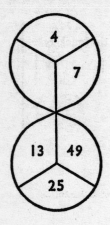

22.   Insert the word missing from the brackets.

worker (roam) amaze
tester (....) omen

23.   Insert a word that means the same as the two words outside the brackets.

weapon (...) tie

24. Underline the odd-man-out.

25. Insert the letter which completes the series.

two T four U three —

26. Insert the missing letter.

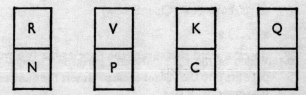

27. Which of the four numbered figures completes the top line?

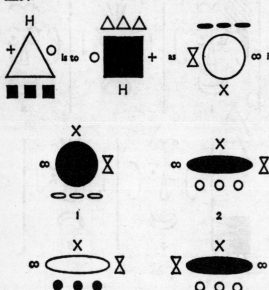

28. Insert the word missing from the bracket.

BEDS (DEER) FREE

LEFT (....) BRAN

29. Insert the word that completes the first word and starts the second. (Clue: Sheep.)

T (...) P

30. Which of the six numbered figures on the opposite page fits into the vacant square? (Insert the number in the square.)

31. Insert the missing letter.

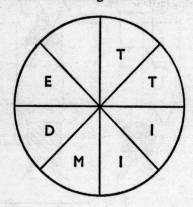

32. Insert the missing number.

```
7   14   12
4   12    9
6   24   —
```

33. Underline which of these words is unlike the others.

sash   German   bow   French

34. Insert the missing number.

35. Insert the missing letters.

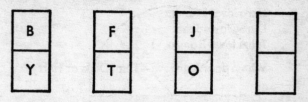

36. Which of the six numbered figures is the next figure in the series? Underline the answer.

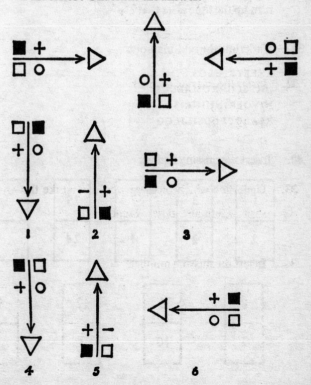

37. Underline the name which completes the fourth line.

Hero loves Leander
Darby loves Joan
Juliet loves Romeo

Whom does Joan love – Tom, Dick, or Harry?

38. I was supposed to meet my girl friend at noon every Sunday. The first time she came at 12.30, the next time at 1.20, then at 2.30, then at 4.00. When did she turn up the time after that?

39. Underline the odd-man-out.

AZEETRIULOS
OHEELORRUMAELUS
NIVOERINNIURIS
REALOPPOOSILILOO

40. Insert the missing figures.

1	3	7	19	
2	2	4	24	

TEST FOUR

1. Insert the missing number.

36 30 24 18 —

2. Underline the odd-man-out.

Byron Shelley Keats Chamberlain Chaucer

3. Which of the six numbered figures fits into the vacant square? (Insert the number in the square.)

4. Insert the missing number.

4 9 17 35 ___ 139

5. Underline which of these cities is the odd-man-out.

Shanghai   Lhasa
Delhi   Cairo
New Orleans   Quebec

6. Underline which of these is not a football team.

SHAELEC
NESARLA
ANTIGS
OLATSNALIV
LOVESW

7. Insert the word missing from the brackets.

floor-covering (carpeting) telling off
container (. . .) shock

8. Insert the missing number.

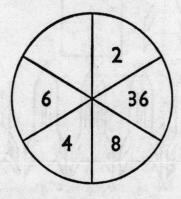

9. Which of the six numbered figures fits into the vacant square? (Insert the number in the square.)

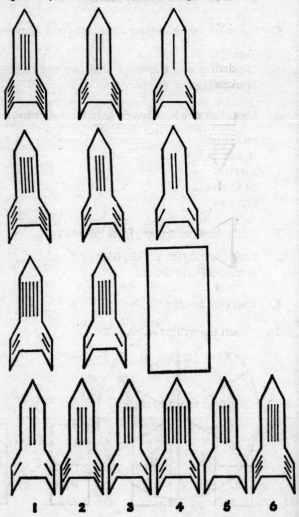

10. Insert the word that completes the first word and starts the second. (Clue: Learn.)

s (....) p

11. Underline which two of these six drawings do not make a pair.

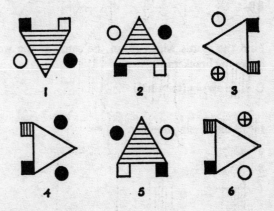

1 2 3

4 5 6

12. Insert the missing letter.

D K G N _ Q M T

13. Insert the missing number.

16	28	41	58
37	49	62	

14. Insert the word in the brackets that can be prefixed by any of the letters on the left.

15. Find the words which mean the same as the words inside the brackets.

C + (crow) = (criminal)

16. Insert the missing number.

9 4 20
8 5 12
7 6 —

17. Underline the odd-man-out.

Enterprise: tripe, peer, rite, rent, print, pair, rips

18. Insert the word that completes the first word and starts the second. (Clue: Search.)

CON (. . . . .) ION

19. Which of the six numbered figures on the opposite page fits into the vacant square below? (Insert the number in the square.)

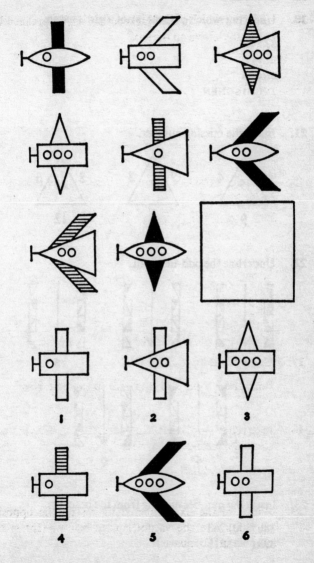

20. Underline which of these is not a girl's name.

SAYDI
BLISY
SHOLT
TEEMILCNEN

21. Insert the missing number.

22. Underline the odd-man-out.

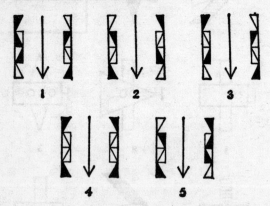

23. Insert the number missing from the brackets.

188 (300) 263
893 (   ) 915

24. Insert a word that means the same as the two words outside the brackets.

change (. . . . . .) rod

25. Complete the following from the five numbered figures. (Underline the correct figure.)

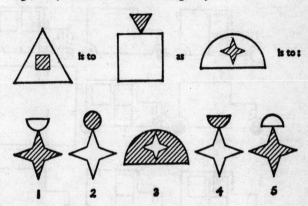

26. Underline which of these is not a film star.

BALEG
RAYLOT
OROPEC
PALSREM
DABTOR

27. Insert the missing letter.

S P L
O K F
U P —

28. Which of the six numbered figures fits into the vacant square? (Insert the number in the square.)

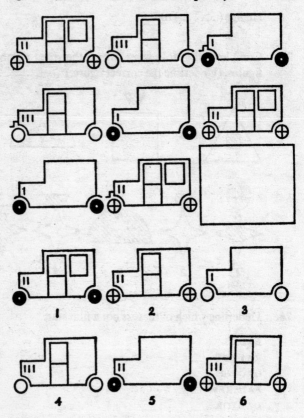

29. Insert the number missing from the brackets.

347 (418) 489
643 (   ) 721

30. Which of the six numbered figures is the next in the series? (Underline the correct figure.)

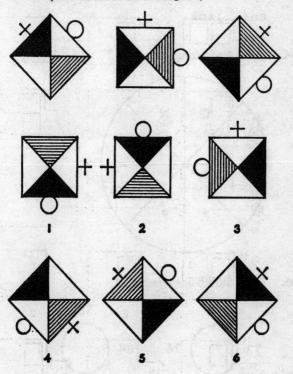

1   2   3

4   5   6

31. Insert the missing number.

```
4   12   10   6
10   3    6   7
6    8   __   5
```

32. Underline the odd-man-out.

aplomb   foreboding   moan   redress   willow

33. Insert the word that completes the first word and starts the second. (Clue: Weapon.)

CH(...)ADA

34. Insert the missing letter.

35. Insert the missing number.

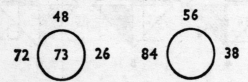

36. Insert the missing letters.

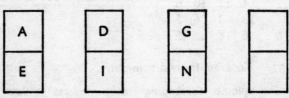

37. Insert the word that completes the first word and starts the second. (Clue: Quietude.)

FO (....) IVE

38. Underline the phrase which completes the sequence.

Alfred had his cakes; Bruce had his spider; Canute had his waves. Which comes next: Charles with his Nell; John with his barons; Keats with his poetry; Henry with his wives; or Richard with his hunchback?

39. Insert the letter to complete the series.

C V H O Q __

40. Insert the missing number.

14	10	12	16
84	40	60	

TEST FIVE

1. Insert the missing letter.

A D G J __

2. Underline the odd-man-out.

Rembrandt Shakespeare Tintoretto Raphael Monet

3. Which of the six numbered figures fits into the vacant square? (Insert the number in the square.)

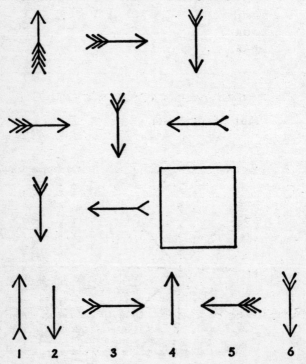

4. Insert the missing number.

2   5   9   19   37   __

5. Underline which of these animals is the odd-man-out.

herring   porpoise   shark   ray   sole   plaice

6. Underline which of these towns is in England.

RINLEB
RETHISCEHC
DADRIM
MORE

7. Insert the word missing from the brackets.

strap (. . . .) orchestra

8. Insert the number missing from the top of the drawing.

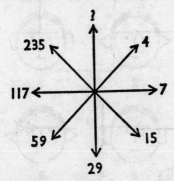

9. Which of the six numbered figures fits into the vacant square? (Insert the number in the square.)

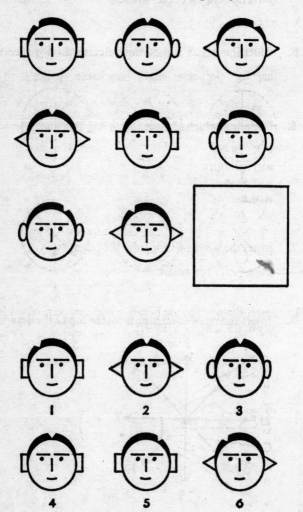

10. Insert the word that completes the first word and starts the second. (Clue: Music.)

BLES (. . . .) LET

11. Underline which two of these figures do not form a pair.

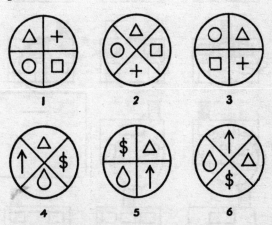

12. Insert the word in the brackets that can be prefixed by any of the letters on the left.

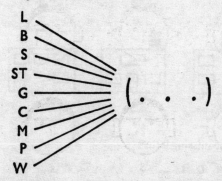

13. Which of the six numbered figures fits into the vacant square? (Insert the number in the square.)

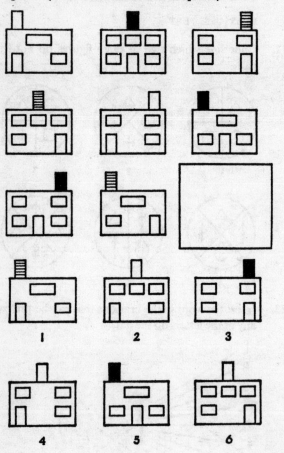

1   2   3

4   5   6

14. Insert the missing letter.

N O M Q I —

15. Find the words which mean the same as the words inside the brackets.

N + (exit) = (female)

16. Insert the missing number.

4 6 3 8
2 8 4 4
6 5 __ 10

17. Underline the word from the bottom line that goes with the three at the top.

PLANE SHORE BREEZE
rot lily cat able dog fool

18. Underline which of these is not an animal.

LATHPEEN
TICRECK
HELAW
FEFEOC

19. Insert the missing number.

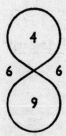 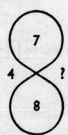

20. Insert the word that completes the first word and starts the second. (Clue: Golf.)

S (. . .) E

21. Underline the odd-man-out.

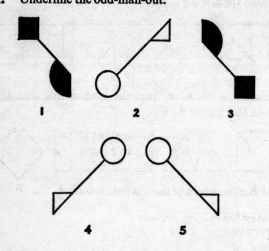

22. Insert the word missing from the brackets.

TE (FEET) 56
EC (. . . .) 94

23. Underline which of these towns is not in England.

NITHGORB
DOLNON
POORLIVEL
SOWGALG
REEXET

24. Insert the word that means the same as the two words outside the brackets.

stake (....) mail

25. Which of the five numbered figures fits into the vacant space? (Insert the number in the square.)

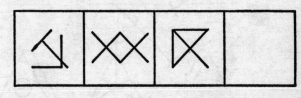

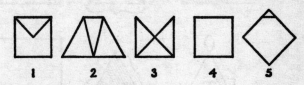

26. Insert the missing number.

3 7 15 31 —

27. Insert the missing letters.

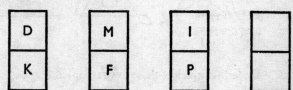

28. Insert the word missing from the brackets.

astringent (sale) eldorado
affect (....) embargo

29. Which of the six numbered figures fits into the vacant square? (Insert the number in the square.)

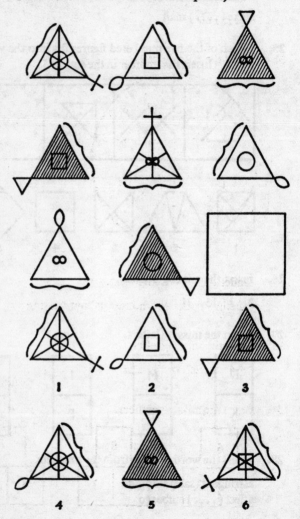

30. Insert the word that completes the first word and starts the second. (Clue: Clean.)

G (. . .) Y

31. Insert the missing letter.

32. Underline the odd-man-out.

captain   frustrate   house   labour   swing

33. Insert the missing letter.

C 4 K 2 O 3 __

34. Insert the missing number.

35. Insert the missing number.

```
 6   8   7
36  64  49
24  48  __
```

36. Underline which of the four numbered figures fits into the empty space.

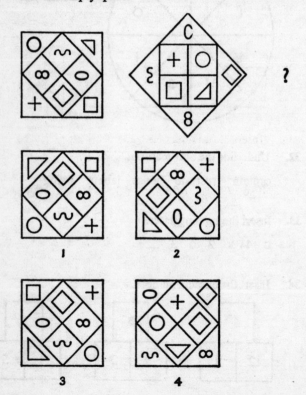

37. At a séance, the medium conjured up Bismarck, Disraeli, Fox, and Hastings. Whom did she conjure up next: Pitt, Marlborough, Jeffreys, More, or Wellington? Underline the correct word.

38. Underline the odd-man-out.

739   1341   522   1862

39. Insert the missing number.

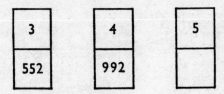

40. Insert the missing number.

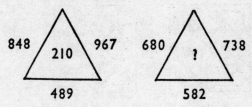

TEST SIX

1. Which of the six numbered figures fits into the vacant square? (Insert the number in the square.)

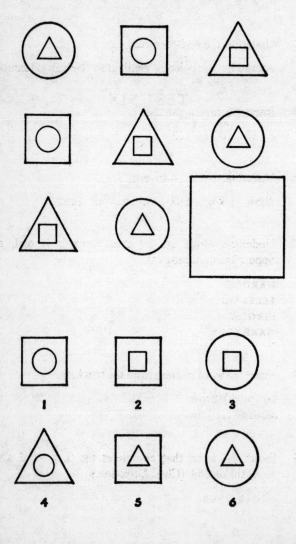

2. Find the missing letter.

F J N R __

3. Underline the odd-man-out.

Alexander Napoleon Wellington Nelson Hannibal

4. Insert the missing number.

8 12 10 16 12 __

5. Underline the odd-man-out.

dhow packet rickshaw barque junk

6. Underline which one of these animals is real, as opposed to mythological.

NARDOG
FELERWOW
FIRGINF
GAARNOOK

7. Insert the word missing from the brackets.

tar (pitch) throw
saloon (...) rod

8. Insert the word that completes the first word and starts the second. (Clue: Direction.)

GRO (..) PER

9. Which of the six numbered figures fits into the vacant square ? (Insert the number in the square.)

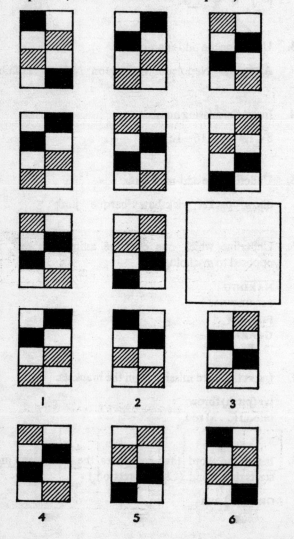

10. Insert the missing number.

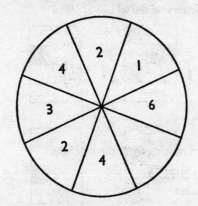

11. Underline the odd-man-out.

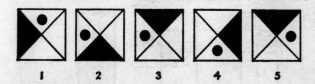

12. Insert the missing letter.

H K Q
C G O
E J —

13. Underline the domino which is the odd-man-out.

2	5	3	4	1
3	7	6	8	7

14. Insert the word in the brackets which can be prefixed by any of the letters on the left.

H
B
P
W
ST
(. . . .)

15. Insert the word missing from the brackets.

paper (weight) lifter
sheep (. . .) collar

16. Insert the missing number.

6		10		14
12				22
19		25		31

17. Underline the odd-man-out.

Accessory: sear, race, sore, cross, fare, rose, core, case, aces

18. Insert the word that completes the first word and starts the second. (Clue: Law.)

DUR (...) GAIN

19. Which of the six numbered figures fits into the vacant square? (Insert the number in the square.)

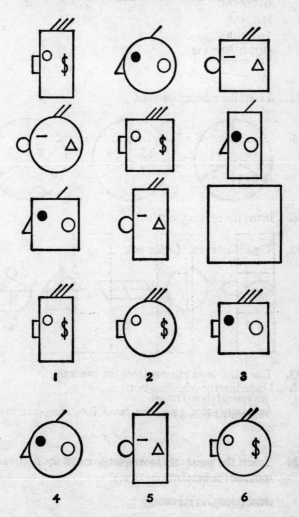

20. Underline which of these towns is not in the U.S.A.

GICOHAC
SHENAT
TONSOB
GOTHNINSAW

21. Insert the missing number.

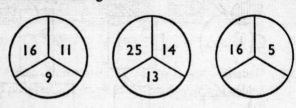

22. Underline the odd-man-out.

23. Insert the word missing from the brackets.

gravyboat (boss) russet
suspenders (. . . .) leper

24. Insert the word that means the same as the two words outside the bracket.

excursion (. . . . .) energy

25. Underline which of the five numbered figures fits into the empty space.

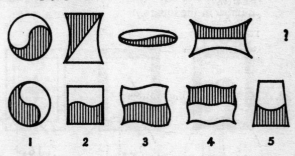

26. Underline which of the animals whose names are hidden in the jumbled letters below has less than four feet.

TAR
NOIL
ETHALPEN
SORBASALT
GUAJAR

27. Insert the number missing from the brackets.

164 (225) 286
224 (   ) 476

28. Insert the word that completes the first word and starts the second. (Clue: Spring.)

RE (....) IL

29. Underline the odd-man-out.

837   612   549   422   342

30. Which of the six numbered figures on the opposite page fits into the vacant square below? (Insert the number in the square.)

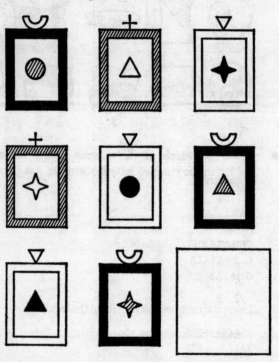

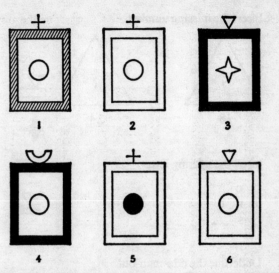

31.   Insert the missing number.

       8   3   21
       6   5   25
      12   2   —

32.   Insert the word missing from the brackets.

       54 (fade) 16
       58 (....) 31

33.   Underline the odd-man-out.

       chair   bed   playpen   table   couch

34. Insert the missing number.

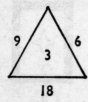

35. Insert the missing letter.

L O T
D H O
P S __

36. Underline the odd-man-out.

9 25 36 78 144 196

37. Insert the missing letter.

B	G	N	P
F	M	V	

38. Insert the missing number.

7 15 32 __ 138 281

39. BAGG is to William the Conqueror as BEJC is to whom?

40. Insert the missing number.

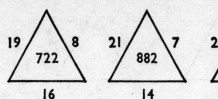

TEST SEVEN

1. Insert the missing letter.

   R O L I __

2. Underline the odd-man-out.

   Mozart Bach Socrates Handel Beethoven

3. Insert the missing number.

   17 19 __ 20 15

4. Underline which of these towns is the odd-man-out.

   Oslo London New York Cairo Bombay Caracas
   Madrid

5. Disentangle the letters in each of these words, all of
   which are names of animals. Underline which animal
   is the largest.

   LARPODE
   RHOSE
   SNUKK
   GITER
   EARZB
   OMSEO
   ARBTIB

6. Insert the word that completes the first word and
   starts the second. (Clue: Through.)

   ROM (. . .) SON

7. Which of the six numbered figures fits into the vacant square? (Insert the number in the square.)

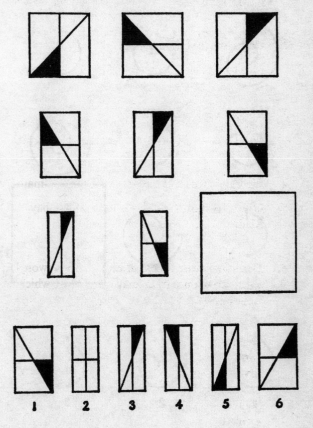

8. Insert the word missing from the brackets.

plank (board) meals
strike (. . .) success

9. Which of the six numbered figures fits into the vacant square? (Insert the number in the square.)

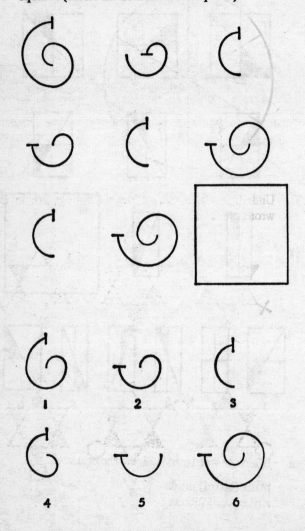

10. Insert the missing number.

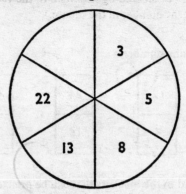

11. Underline which two of these drawings are in the wrong order.

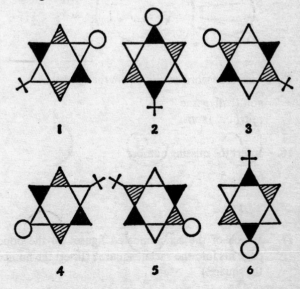

12. Insert the missing letter.

D   H   L   R   __

13. Insert the missing number.

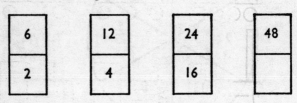

14. Insert the word in the brackets that can be prefixed by any of the letters on the left.

15. Insert the word missing from the brackets.

golf (ball) game
rain (...) sprit

16. Insert the missing number

6   4   5
3   2   1
8   5   __

17. Which of the six numbered figures on the opposite page fits into the vacant square? (Insert the number in the square.)

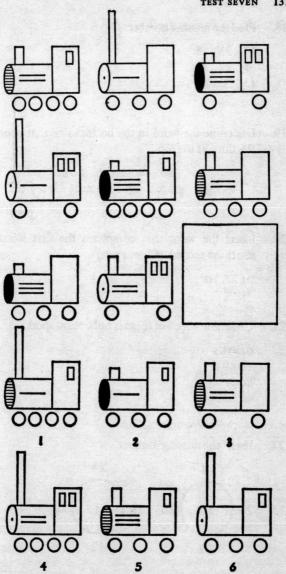

18. Find the missing number.

```
17  33   8
 5  29  12
13  __  10
```

19. Underline the word in the bottom line that goes with the three at the top.

ROVER   FALL   LORD

tiger   grace   slip   moment   fear   car

20. Insert the word that completes the first word and starts the second. (Clue: Past.)

D(...)G

21. Underline which of these is not a team sport.

GINIKS

YGBUR

LOOP

LALOTBOF

22. Insert the missing number.

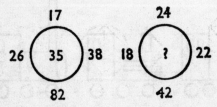

23. Underline the odd-man-out.

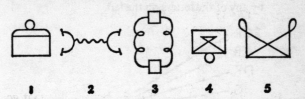

24. Insert the word missing from the brackets.

ardour (rain) ninety
oppression (. . . .) trappings

25. Insert the word that means the same as the two words outside the brackets.

smart (. . . . .) bulge.

26. Which of the five numbered figures fits into the vacant square? (Insert the number in the square.)

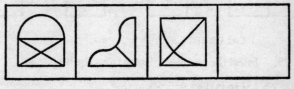

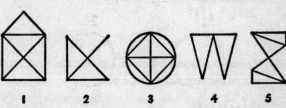

27. Insert the word in the brackets which can be prefixed by any of the letters on the left.

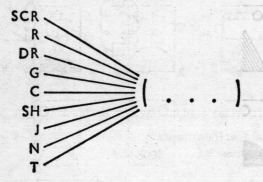

SCR
R
DR
G
C
SH
J
N
T

(. . .)

28. Insert the missing number and letter.

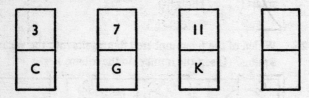

3	7	II	
C	G	K	

29. Insert the number missing from the brackets.

132 (834) 285
214 (   ) 117

30. Insert the word which completes the first word and starts the second. (Clue: Dark.)

κ (. . . . .) IE

31. Which of the six numbered figures fits into the vacant square? (Insert the number in the square.)

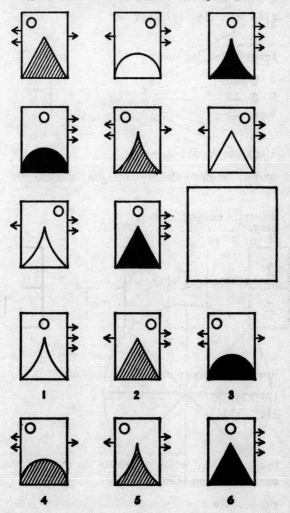

32. Underline which of these numbers does not belong with the others.

625   361   256   197   144

33. Insert the missing number.

4   8   20
9   3   15
6   6   —

34. Underline the odd-man-out.

animal   engine   identity   octagon   unicorn

35. Insert the missing number.

4   6   9   14   —

36. Insert the missing letter.

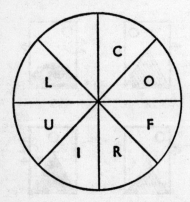

37. Insert the word that completes the first word and
starts the second. (Clue: Insect.)

CH (. . .) HEM

38. Insert the missing number

28   33   31   36   34   __

39. Insert the missing number.

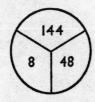

40. If DGJ + JAE + BHF = DDAB, and $\dfrac{F \times C}{J} = $ GA,

what is $\dfrac{A}{G}$?

TEST EIGHT

1. Insert the missing letter.

   W   S   O   K   ——

2. Underline the odd-man-out.

   August   September   October   November   December

3. Insert the missing number.

   36   28   24   22   ——

4. Underline the odd-man-out.

   Spain   Denmark   Germany   France   Italy   Finland

5. Disentangle the letters in each of these words, all of which are names of different types of vehicles. Underline which one is unlike the others.

   RACT
   KRCUT
   BLEICCY
   LEGSIH
   CARGIARE

6. Insert the word that means the same as the two words outside the brackets.

   fowl (......) grumble

7. Insert the word that completes the first word and starts the second. (Clue: Profit.)

   BAR (....) SAY

8. Which of the six numbered figures fits into the vacant square? (Insert the number in the square.)

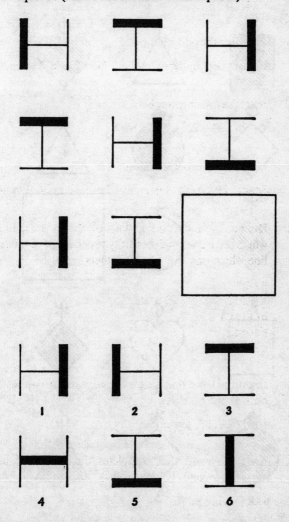

9. Which of the six numbered figures fits into the vacant square? (Insert the number in the square.)

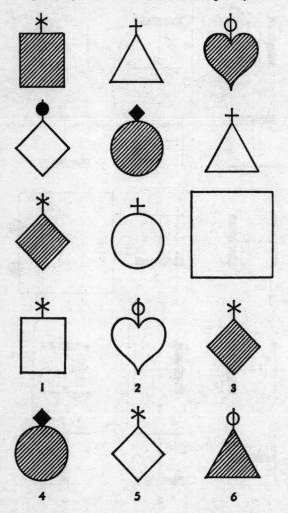

10. Insert the missing number.

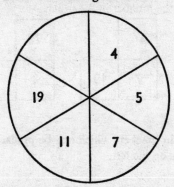

11. Underline the odd-man-out.

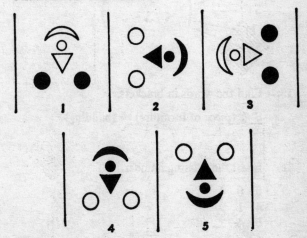

12. Insert the missing letter.

K N E
M O I
T X —

13. Insert the missing number.

14. Insert the word in brackets which can be prefixed by any of the letters on the left.

TH
L
ST —— (. . .)
M
W

15. Find the words in brackets.

S + (piece of furniture) = (building)

16. Insert the missing number.

8 6 4
4 1 9
6 4 —

17. Which of the six numbered figures on the opposite page fits into the vacant space? (Insert the number in the space.)

18. Underline which of the words in the second row belongs with those in the first row.

      RAT BIRD CART COLOUR
      rain lily animal light paper

19. Insert the word that completes the first word and starts the second. (Clue: Nuisance.)

TEM (....) LES

20. Underline which of these towns is not in Italy.

NORLEFEC
DARDIM
SAIP
LIMNA

21. Insert the missing number.

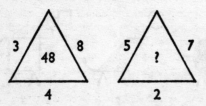

22. Underline the odd-man-out.

   1   2   3   4   5

23. Insert the number missing from the brackets.

   243 (222) 317
   548 (   ) 621

24. Insert a word that means the same as the two words outside the brackets.

   stick (. . . . .) wager

25. Which of the five numbered figures fits into the empty space? (Insert the number.)

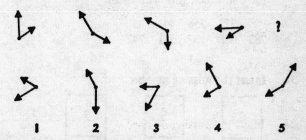

   1   **2**   **3**   **4**   **5**

26. Insert the missing letter.

   D R I G
   T R I D
   D R I __

27. Insert the missing letters.

D	H	L	
W	S	O	

28. Insert the word missing from the brackets.

policeman (Mars) nurse
solicitor (. . . .) barrister

29. Insert the word which completes the first word and starts the second. (Clue: Male.)

UR (. . . .) LE

30. Here are three numbers; underline, from those below, the one which goes with them.

372 258 441
283 488 137 381 242

31. Insert the missing number.

8	5	9
26	20	
13	16	12

32. Insert the missing number.

5 6 7 8 10 11 14 __

33. Which of the six numbered figures on the opposite page fits into the vacant circle? (Insert the number in the circle.)

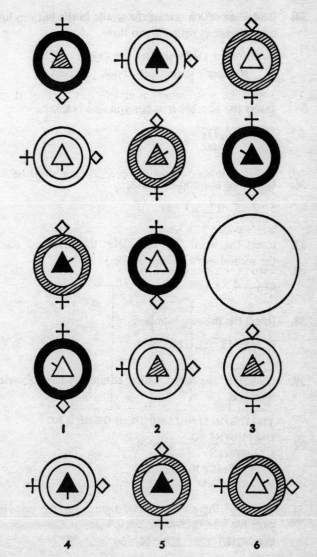

1   2   3

4   5   6

34. Underline which one of the words in the bottom line below belongs with the top three.

LAND   NIGHT   WATER
weather   grace   pit   book   serpent

35. Insert the number missing from the brackets.

532 (630) 217
648 (   ) 444

36. Underline the odd-man-out.

5   7   9   17   23   37

37. Insert the word that completes the first and starts the second word. (Clue: To be.)

ST (...) NA

38. Insert the missing number.

8   24   12   ___   18   54

39. Underline the word which completes the following sentence.

THRIPGUH is to ALMOOW as GUMP is to:
GLITHGINRYO
UDLOTWIN
TIPSYCHATRY
CHASTIPLAW

40. Insert the missing number.

260   216   128   108   62   54   ___   27

ANSWERS AND EXPLANATIONS

Test One

1. 14. (Numbers go up by three each time.)

2. Office. (People don't live in an office.)

3. 14 and 13. (There are two alternate series, going up by two each.)

4. Whale. (It is a mammal, the others are fish.)

5. Comet. (Ford, Vanguard, Bentley, and Fiat are makes of cars; the Comet is an airliner.)

6. Ball. (The word in the middle has the same meaning as the two words at either side; a dance is a ball, and a ball is a sphere.)

7. LET

8. 5. (Figures get smaller, progressing from left to right.)

9. 3. (Each line contains a circle, a square, and a diamond; the diagrams are alternately up-and-down or sideways. The missing figure must therefore be a square with up-and-down lines inside.)

10. 32. (Multiply the first number by the second to get the third: $1 \times 2 = 2$; then multiply the second and third numbers to get the fourth, and so on. $4 \times 8 = 32$, so that 32 is the missing number.) *Or* 8. (Numbers on left are $4 \times$ their opposites.)

11. 5. (The solid line goes round in a counter-clockwise direction, the solid circle in a clockwise direction, and the two cross-strokes precede the circle, except in 5, where they follow it.)

12.

18
30

(The numbers at the top follow the sequence −1, +2, −3, +4; those at the bottom: +1, −2, +3, −4.)

13. v. (In the alphabetical sequence, skip two and three letters alternately.)

14. INCH.

15. Ram and dram. (A ram is a male sheep, and a dram is a small draught of spirit.)

16. 6. (Each number in the bottom row is half the sum of the numbers in the other two rows.)

17. Time. (All these words can be prefixed by 'life'.)

18. 3. (There are in each row and column three types of face (round, square, and triangular), noses are either black, white, or stippled, eyes are white, black, or half-and-half, and there are either one, two, or three hairs. The missing face must therefore be square, with a black nose, three hairs, and one black and one white eye.)

19. PIN.

20. Sabrina. (The poets are Keats, Byron, Chaucer, and Wordsworth.)

21. 6. (Add the figures at the ends of the long arrows, and subtract from this the figures at the ends of the short arrows.)

22. GALLANT. (Substitute the four letters outside the brackets for the sixth, fifth, third, and second missing letter, in that order.)

23. Grub.

24. 5. (At each turn the small circle and square change places; they fail to do so on the last occasion, so that 5 is the odd-man-out. Arrow and ? stay in their places throughout.)

25. Salome. (The composers are Mozart, Strauss, and Verdi.)

26. D. (The letter in the second column is always as many letters below that in the first column as the letter in the third column is above that in the first column. Thus N is four letters below I, and D is four letters above I.)

27. 2. (As the square with the circle inside becomes a circle with a rotated square inside, so the triangle with the square inside becomes a square with a rotated triangle inside. The cross-hatching is transferred from the inner figure to the outer figure. The three outside rectangles are turned upside-down, and those that were cross-hatched become black, while those that were black become cross-hatched.)

28. 2. (The main figure is rotated through 90 degrees. Cross-hatched and white areas are interchanged, and the central figure is rotated independently through 90 degrees.)

29. RAIN. (The word in brackets is made up of the last but two and last but three letters (in that order) of the word before the brackets, and of the same letters of the word after the brackets.)

30. TOP.

31. 3. (All the original figures have either three lines with a right-angle, or six lines without one.)

32. 1. (In each row and column there is a round, square, and thin body; round, square, and thin feet; round, square,

and triangular head; and raised, lowered, or level arms.
The missing man must therefore have a thin body, round
feet, a square head, and lowered arms.)

33. 10. (The number in the last column is the sum of the
numbers in the first two columns minus the number in the
third column. $(13 + 8) - 11 = 10.$)

34. New York. (New York is not a capital city.)

35. 18. (Multiply the three numbers outside the triangle with
each other, and divide by ten.)

36.

E
H

(There are two chains, beginning with A and D
respectively, and jumping one letter each time;
these chains go up and down alternately, i.e.
A at the top is followed by C at the bottom, etc.)

37. BEAT.

38. 26. (There are two alternate series, starting with the first
two numbers, and each formed by doubling the preceding
number in its own series and subtracting 2. $2 \times 14 = 28$;
$28 - 2 = 26.$)

39. O. (The number of letters between A and each successive
letter in the series is always a *prime*, going up in order from
2 through 3, 5, 7, 11 to 13. There are thirteen letters
between A and O.)

40. 238. (The series is formed by starting with the number 3,
and then forming each successive part of the series by
taking the first, second, third, fourth, and fifth powers of 3,
and subtracting respectively 1, 2, 3, 4, and 5.) $3^1 - 1 = 2$;
$3^2 - 2 = 7$; $3^3 - 3 = 24$; $3^4 - 4 = 77$; $3^5 - 5 = 238.$)

Test Two

1. 24. (Numbers go up by four each time.)

2. 3. (Dots decrease by one in each direction.)

3. Herring. (It is the only fish among mammals.)

4. 90 and 93. (The series is formed by alternately adding three and doubling the preceding number; thus $45 \times 2 = 90$, and $90 + 3 = 93$.)

5. Apollo. (He is the only Greek god among Roman ones.)

6. Washington. (Athens, Moscow, Milan, and Wigan are in Europe.)

7. Blow. (The word in the middle has the same meaning as the two words at either side; a hit is a blow, and to blow is to puff.)

8. APE.

9. 5. (The figures in the bottom row are the same as in the top row, with black and white reversed.)

10. z. (D is the third letter from A, H the fourth from D, M the fifth from H, s the sixth from M, and z the seventh from s.)

11. 39. (Each number, beginning with 3, is double the preceding one minus one, minus two, minus three, etc. $22 \times 2 = 44; 44 - 5 = 39$.)

12. 4. (1 and 3 form a pair, and so do 2 and 5. In each pair one figure has been rotated through 90 degrees, and the black and white shading have been interchanged. Figure 4 does not fit into this.)

13. 22. (To get the bottom number in each domino, double the top number and subtract one, two, three, and four for the first, second, third, and fourth domino. 13 × 2 = 26; 26 − 4 = 22.)

14. ART *or* ARE *or* ILL.

15. Ball. (The word in brackets provides a bridge between the one before and the one after the brackets; it can terminate the first and begin the second.)

16. 4. (There are three head-shapes, three body-shapes, three types of tail, and one, two, or three whiskers. Each occurs only once in each row and column.)

17. 13. (Add the first and last number in each row to get the centre one.)

18. Sink. (In all the other words the last two letters are consecutive letters in the alphabet; not so in 'sink'.)

19. BIT.

20. Sparrow. (The islands are Cuba, Ireland, and Capri.)

21. 16. (Take the number at the top, divide by that on the right, and double the result.)

22. 2. (1 and 5 are identical, so are 3 and 4.)

23. Face. (The numbers refer to the respective letters of the alphabet, i.e. 5 is E, the fifth letter, etc. These letters are then substituted for the numbers, and read in reverse order.)

24. Rook. (A rook is a kind of crow, and to rook is to swindle.)

25. 786. (The numbers after the word 'Scotland' correspond to the letters of that word; the words 'lots', 'loan', and 'and' are made up from the letters in 'Scotland', and the numbers after them are the numbers corresponding to these letters in the original word, with 1 added to each number after 'lots', 2 added after 'loan', and 3 added after 'and'.)

26. H. (The number of letters in the alphabet which lie between successive letters in the question are 2, 4, 6, 8, 10, and 12, and the direction alternates from forward to backward along the alphabet (i.e. from A to Z, and then from Z to A). Alternative explanation: Alternate letters go two steps down the alphabet and two steps up; the sequence N, L, J, leads to H as the next letter).

27. 2. (The original circle is halved, and the original square turned through an angle of 45 degrees and put on top of the half-circle; similarly the large square is halved to make a rectangle, and the diamond in it turned through an angle of 45 degrees and put on top of the rectangle. In addition, cross-hatching in the original figure is omitted in the second one, and vice versa.)

28. SLIP. (The letters in front of the brackets are the letters which in the alphabet are just in front of the first two letters of the word in the bracket, while those behind the bracket are the letters which in the alphabet are just behind the last two letters of the word in the brackets. R is before S, K is before L; J is after I, and Q is after P.)

29. END *or* ALL.

30. 1. (Each cross outside the square counts *plus* one, each cross inside *minus* one; in the bottom row +3 — 1 = + 2. Consequently there are two crosses outside the square in the answer.)

31. 2. (It has no right-angles.)

32. 2. (All the rows and columns add up to thirty; 12 + 16 = 28, thus a two is required to make up the thirty.)

33. Steamer. (The other three words are colloquially connected with three nationalities – Dutch courage, French leave, German measles; steamer is not.)

34. 52. (In the second figure, the numbers are half of those in the first figure; in the third they are twice those in the first figure. The missing one must therefore be 26 × 2 = 52. The positions of the numbers do not correspond, but shift one position each time).

35.

6
S

(Numbers increase by one each time; the letter is as many places in the alphabet away from the preceding one as is indicated by the number above it. Thus H is four places away from D; M five places from H, and s six places from M.)

36. Sex. (Concupiscence is sexual appetite.)

37. ACE.

38. Reverse. (A palimpsest is a manuscript the original writing in which has been erased so that it can be used again; a palindrome is a word or phrase which reads the same even when it is reversed, e.g. OTTO.)

39. J. (Numbered consecutively, the letters are 2, 5, 10, 17, and 26. These numbers are the squares of the first five numbers (1, 2, 3, 4, 5) with one added each time. $3^2 = 9; 9 + 1 = 10$, and the tenth letter is J.)

40. 5436. (There are two series, beginning respectively with 7 and 9, and going on to alternate numbers. For the one series, square 7 and subtract the figure immediately following 7, i.e.; $7^2 - 9 = 40$. Similarly, $40^2 - 74 = 1526$. For the other series, square 9 and subtract the figure immediately before 9, i.e. 7; $9^2 - 7 = 74$. To get the missing number, square 74 and subtract 40; this gives 5436.)

Test Three

1. 5. (Numbers go down by five each time.)

2. Sleigh. (It has no wheels.)

3. 74. (Each number is twice the preceding one plus one, two, three, and finally four; thus $35 \times 2 + 4 = 74$.)

4. Spider. (It has eight legs; all the others have six.)

5. Mouse. (The other animals are bison, kitten, warthog, and giraffe.)

6. Record. (A disc is a record, and a record is an achievement.)

7. 4. (There are three figures (circle, square, and triangle) in one of three positions each; one is black, the others white.)

8. END.

9. 6. (The sector rotates through 90 degrees counter-clockwise in each column, and clockwise in each row.)

10. E. (There are two alternating series; in the first you jump one, two, three, etc., letters forward, in the other you jump one, two, three, etc., letters backwards. Jumping three letters back from I takes you to E.

11. 33. (Each number is the preceding one multiplied by two, and with one subtracted from the product; thus 17 × 2 = 34, and 34 − 1 = 33.)

12. 4. (White ovals have arrows attached to them pointing right or up; black ovals have arrows pointing left or down. Oval 4 is black, but has an arrow pointing up.)

13.

7
13

(Top numbers increase by 2, 3, 4, 5; bottom numbers by twice that, i.e. 4, 6, 8, 10.)

14. 1. (There are three head-shapes, and three types of nose, mouth, and eyebrow; each only occurs once in each row and column.)

15. AND.

16. Horn. (The word in brackets provides a bridge between the one in front and the one behind the brackets; it can terminate the first and begin the second.)

17. 19. (To find the third number in each row, subtract the second from the first.)

18. Police. (In all the other words, the first and second letters are consecutive letters in the alphabet; in 'police' this order is reversed).

19. CHIEF.

20. Venus. (The boys' names are Robert, Benedict, and William.)

21. 97. (Go round the figure eight in a clockwise direction, starting with the 4; each number is twice the preceding one, minus one. 49 × 2 = 98 − 1 = 97.)

22. SEEM. (The word in brackets is made up of the third and second letters, in that order, of the words on either side of the brackets.)

23. Bow.

24. 4. (1 and 3 are identical, so are 2 and 5.)

25. H. (T is the first letter in the word 'two', U is the third letter in 'four', and H is the second letter in 'three'. The number of the letter is thus always one less than the number spelled out in the question.)

26. G. (The bottom letter is four, six, eight, and ten places in the alphabet back from the top letter.)

27. 2. (The three identical small figures below the large figure become the main figure, while the original main figure is changed into three small figures which now go to the opposite side. The three small figures right, left, and above the main figure change positions. Figures black or white in the first drawing remain black or white in the second.)

28. FEAR. (The word in the bracket is formed from the second and third letters of the words outside the bracket, taken in reverse.)

29. RAM.

30. 6. (In each row and column there are three kinds of body (round, square, and triangular), three kinds of head (also round, square, and triangular), three types of tail (straight, waved, and curly,) three types of leg (line, black, and

white.) In addition, the bodies are either white, black, or shaded. The missing chicken must therefore be as number 6.)

31. E. (The letters, read clockwise, spell 'time' and 'tide' when read alternately.)

32. 20. (The number in the last column is formed by subtracting from the number in the second column a number x. x is the number which shows how many times the number in the first column has to be multiplied to give the number in the second column. $4 \times 6 = 24$; $24 - 4 = 20$.)

33. German. (The other three words can prefix the word window; German cannot.)

34. 14. (There are two series, one of odd and the other of even numbers. Both go up by two each time, and they alternate position; i.e. being up or down.)

35.

N
J

(The letters at the top advance by skipping three letters of the alphabet, those at the bottom go back in the alphabet and skip four.)

36. 1. (The arrow, the triangle, and the black and white squares are turned through an angle of 90 degrees each time. The cross and the circle follow suit, but change places with each other on each occasion.)

37. Tom. (The first letters in the names of the lovers are three, five, and seven letters apart; Joan and Tom continue the series and are nine letters apart.)

38. 5.50. (The first time she was 30 minutes late, the second time 30 + 50 minutes, the third time 30 + 50 + 70

minutes, then 30 + 50 + 70 + 90 minutes, and finally
30 + 50 + 70 + 90 + 110 minutes.)

39. NIVOERINNIURIS. (Zeus, Hermes, and Apollo are Greek
gods, Venus is Roman. These gods are hidden and can be
recovered by counting only those letters preceded by a
vowel not forming part of their names.)

40.

115
576

(The series begins with $\frac{1}{2}$. For successive values,
add 1, 2, 3, 4 respectively. Divide each resulting
value by 1×1, 1×2, $1 \times 2 \times 3$, $1 \times 2 \times 3$
$\times 4$.)

Test Four

1. 12. (Numbers go down by six each time.)

2. Chamberlain. (He was not a poet.)

3. 2. (Arms are up, down, or sideways, and heads are white,
black, or shaded once in each row and column.)

4. 69. (Each number is twice the preceding one, with 1 added
or subtracted from alternate numbers. $2 \times 35 = 70 - 1$
$= 69$.)

5. Quebec. (All the other towns are in roughly the same
latitude; Quebec is much farther north.)

6. Giants. (Arsenal, Chelsea, Aston Villa, and Wolves are
football teams, Giants is a baseball team.)

7. Jar. (The word in the middle has the same meaning as the
two words at either side; a jar is a container, and to jar is
to shock.)

8. 64. (Numbers opposite each other are always squares of one another; the square of 8 is 64.)

9. 5. (The number of lines inside the rocket decreases along the rows; the number of lines in the fins does likewise.)

10. CRAM.

11. 2 and 4. (1 and 5, and 3 and 6, are pairs; you get the one by turning the other through 180 degrees. 2 and 4 do not fit in.)

12. J. (There are two alternating series of letters; in each two letters are skipped. Skipping H and I after G gives J.)

13. 79. (The difference between the two numbers in each set is always twenty-one; the lower one is always larger. Thus 58 + 21 = 79.)

14. EACH.

15. Rook and crook. (C + rook = crook.)

16. 4. (In each row, subtract the second number from the first and multiply by four. 7 − 6 = 1 × 4 = 4.)

17. Pair. (All the other words can be made out of the letters of the word 'enterprise'.)

18. QUEST.

19. 1. (There are three body forms, three wing forms, one, two, or three places in the cockpit, and wings are either white, black, or shaded. Each only occurs once in each row and column.)

20. Sloth. (Daisy, Sybil, and Clementine are the girls' names.)

21. 21. (Multiply the two numbers at the top, and subtract the one at the bottom. $9 \times 3 = 27 - 6 = 21$.)

22. 4. (1 and 5, and 2 and 3, are complementary with the triangles, which are black in the one, white in the other. 4 does not fit into this scheme. Also in the others the two sides (right and left of the arrows) are complementary; in 4 they are identical.)

23. 88. (The number in brackets is four times the difference between the numbers outside the brackets.)

24. Switch.

25. 4. (The larger figure is turned upside-down and put on top of the smaller figure; the smaller figure becomes larger, and the larger figure smaller; the cross-hatched figure becomes plain, and vice versa.)

26. Marples. (The film stars are Gable, Taylor, Cooper, and Bardot.)

27. J. (The letters in the second column are formed by going back in the alphabet two, three, and four spaces respectively. Those in the third column are formed by going back in the alphabet from the letters in the second column three, four, and five spaces respectively. Five spaces back from P is the letter J.)

28. 4. (In each row and column there is one car with solid wheels, one with white wheels, and one with a cross in the wheel. There may be one, two, or three slits in the bonnet. There may be a door and a window, only a door, or neither. And there may be a starting handle, or mudguards, or neither. The answer has to fit into this pattern.)

29. 682. (The number in brackets is half the sum of the numbers outside the brackets.)

30. 1. (The large square rotates counter-clockwise through 45 degrees each time. The cross and the circle rotate through the same angle, but in a clockwise direction.)

31. 9. (The numbers in the third column are made up by adding those in the first and second columns, and subtracting those in the last column. $(6 + 8) - 5 = 9$.)

32. Willow. (In all the other words the first and last letters are consecutive in the alphabet; in willow they are identical.)

33. ARM.

34. R. (The letters, read clockwise, spell out the word 'prisoner'.)

35. 89. (Halve each of the numbers outside the circle, and add the resulting three numbers.)

36.

| J |
| T |

(At the top, skip two letters each time. At the bottom, skip three, then four, and finally five.)

37. REST.

38. Keats with his poetry. (The number of letters in the names are 6, 5, 6; the next one should have 5 letters again. The number of letters in the things are 5, 6, 5; the next one should have 6 letters again. Only Keats (5 letters) with his poetry (6 letters) fits this rule.)

39.

C	3	F	>	2
V	5	B	>	3
H	8	F	>	3
O	12	B	>	4
Q	17	F	>	5
D	23	B	>	6

D. (Each letter in the series is a certain number of letters removed from the beginning or the end of the alphabet alternately. The number in question begins at 3, and goes up by 2, 3, 4, 5, and finally 6.

40. 112. (In each domino, the lower number is derived from the upper one by squaring it, dividing by two, and then subtracting the upper number. Thus $16^2 = 256$; this divided by 2 = 128, 128 − 16 = 112.)

Test Five

1. M. (Letters jump two places in the alphabet.)

2. Shakespeare. (All the others were painters.)

3. 4. (The arrows turn through 90 degrees clockwise in each row, and lose one tail feather each time.)

4. 75. (Each number is twice the preceding one, with one added and subtracted alternately. Thus 37 is twice 19 minus 1, and 75 is twice 37 plus 1.)

5. Porpoise. (The porpoise is a mammal, all the others are fish.)

6. Chichester. (The others are Berlin, Madrid, and Rome.)

7. Band. (The word in the middle has the same meaning as the two words at either side; a strap is a band and a band is an orchestra.)

8. 469. (Starting with 4, each figure is doubled, and one is
   alternately subtracted or added.)

9. 4. (Ears are either square, round, or triangular, and the
   parting is either right, left, or centre. An example of each
   occurs only once in any row or column.)

10. SING.

11. 2 and 5. (1 and 3, and 4 and 6, form pairs, because you can
    get the one from the other by transposing the four small
    figures inside the circle through 90 degrees; this cannot be
    done with 2 and 5.)

12. ORE.

13. 2. (Chimneys may be right, left, or centre, and they may
    be white, black, or shaded. There may be one, two, three
    windows in the top-floor room, and the door may be left,
    right, or centre. Each occurs only once in any row or
    column.)

14. Y. (Each letter jumps alternately forwards and backwards
    in the alphabet, always doubling the number of letters
    jumped, i.e. 1, 2, 4, 8, 16. The sixteenth letter from I is Y.)

15. Egress and Negress.

16. 3. (Multiply the figures in the first two columns, and divide
    the product by the number in the fourth column; this gives
    the number in the third column. $\frac{5 \times 6}{10} = 3$.)

17. Dog. (All these words can be prefixed by the word 'sea'.)

18. Coffee. (The others are elephant, cricket, and whale.)

19. 14. (Multiply the two figures inside the two circles, and divide by the figure at the left. $\frac{8 \times 7}{4} = 14$.)

20. PAR *or* PIN *or* TOP.

21. 5. (There are two pairs of drawings, 1 and 3, and 2 and 4. These pairs are made up by turning one of them through an angle of 180 degrees. Figure 5 does not fit into this scheme.

22. DICE. (The letters in front of the brackets, in inverse order, are the last two letters of the word in brackets. The fifth and sixth letters of the alphabet, in inverse order, give the first two letters of 'feet', while the ninth and fourth letters of the alphabet, in inverse order, give the first two letters of 'dice'.)

23. Glasgow, which is in Scotland. (The others are Brighton, London, Liverpool, and Exeter.)

24. Post. (A stake is a post and to post is to mail.)

25. 4. (It has four straight lines, like all the original figures.)

26. 63. (Double each number and add one. $31 \times 2 = 62$; $62 + 1 = 63$.)

27.

T
M

(Starting with D and K, the letters form a series by skipping one, two, and three letters. The two series alternate position at top or bottom of the domino respectively; i.e. D, F, I, M, and K, M, P, T.)

28. Fame. (The word in brackets is formed from the first two letters, reversed, of the two words outside the brackets.)

29. 6. (Each triangle may be white, cross-hatched, or with three inner lines. It may contain a square, a circle, or an inverted figure eight. It may have opposite the bracket a cross, an oval, or nothing. And it may have a bracket along any of its three sides. The missing triangle must therefore be as indicated.)

30. RUB.

31. I. (The letters, read counter-clockwise, read 'illusion'.) *Or* *A* (Allusion).

32. Swing. (All the other words have three vowels.)

33. U. (Each letter is twice the number of steps removed from the preceding letter as indicated by the number between the letters; thus K is 2 × 4 steps removed from C, and U 2 × 3 steps from O.)

34. 11. (The number in each set of squares add up to twenty.)

35. 35. (The number in the third row is made up by taking the number in the second row and subtracting twice the number in the first row. 49 − (2 × 7) = 35.)

36. 3. (In going from the first figure to the second the four drawings in the corners of the square are rotated one position clockwise, and the square is put inside the diamond; the drawings in the corners of the diamond are rotated one position counter-clockwise, and the diamond is now outside the square. The position of diamond and square is reversed again for the third figure, and the clockwise and counter-clockwise movement of the drawings in the corners of each are continued.)

37. Jeffreys. (The initial letters of these people advance by two – B D F H, so the next one is J.)

38. 1862. (All the other numbers are third powers of 9, 11, and 8 respectively with ten added to each.)

39. 1560. (The numbers at the bottom are derived from the squares of the numbers 24, 32, and 40, i.e. three numbers which go up by 8 each time. From these squares are subtracted the number 8, multiplied by the number at the top, i.e. 3, 4, or 5 respectively. $40^2 - (5 \times 8) = 1560$.)

40. 216. (Each of the numbers outside the triangle is almost a square. Thus 848 is $29^2 + 7$; 967 is $31^2 + 6$; and 489 is $22^2 + 5$. Multiply $7 \times 6 \times 5$, and you get the figure in the triangle, i.e. 210. $680 = 26^2 + 4$; $738 = 27^2 + 9$; $582 = 24^2 + 6$. $6 \times 4 \times 9 = 216$.)

Test Six

1. 1. (In each row there are a circle, a square, or a triangle both as outer figures and as inner ones.)

2. v. (Letters move three places in the alphabet.)

3. Nelson. (He is the only admiral among generals.)

4. 20. (Alternately double and subtract four and halve and add four.)

5. Rickshaw. (All the others are types of boats.)

6. Kangaroo. (Neither the dragon, the werewolf, nor the griffin are real animals.)

7. Bar. (Pitch means the same as tar and throw, and bar means the same as saloon and rod.)

8. UP.

9. 6. (In each column the black, white and shaded spaces move one square closer.)

10. 8. (Numbers opposite each other are always in pairs, so that one is twice as much as the other. Twice four is eight.)

11. 3. (In all the other drawings the circle is one step removed from the black triangle in a clockwise direction; in figure 3 it is one step removed in a counter-clockwise direction.)

12. T. (The letters in the second column are the third, fourth, and fifth respectively after the letter in the first column; those in the third column are the sixth, eighth, and tenth respectively after those in the second column. In other words, they are twice as many letters removed from those in the second column, as these are from those in the first column.)

13. The last. (The differences between the top and bottom number in the others go up by one, i.e. 1, 2, 3, and 4; the last domino goes up by 2. $7 - 1 = 6$.)

14. ITCH *or* ILLS *or* EARS.

15. Dog. (As paper-weight and weight-lifter go together, so sheep-dog and dog-collar go together.)

16. 17. (The top numbers go up by four, from left to right, those in the middle by five, and those at the bottom by six. $12 + 5 = 17$.)

17. Fare. (All the other words can be made out of letters from the word 'accessory'.)

18. BAR.

19. 2. (In each row and column, there are three shapes of face, three shapes of nose, three types of ears, three types of eyes, and three different numbers of hairs. Each only occurs once in each row, and the proper combination gives the missing profile.)

20. Athens, which is in Greece. (The others are Chicago, Boston, and Washington.)

21. 7. (Add the numbers at top right and top left, and divide by 3. 16 + 5 = 21, 21/3 = 7.)

22. 3. (It is the only one without a vertical line.)

23. Deep. (The word in brackets is made up of the last but three and the last but two letters of the words outside the brackets.)

24. Drive. (A drive into the country is an excursion, and a man with drive is a man full of energy.)

25. 3. (Figures containing a straight line are shaded at the top, others at the bottom.)

26. Albatross. (The others are rat, lion, elephant, and jaguar.)

27. 350. (Add the two numbers outside the brackets, and divide by two.)

28. LENT.

29. 422. (All the other numbers are divisible by nine.)

30. 1. (In each row there is one white frame, one cross-hatched, and one black one. There are three different figures on top of the frames, and three different figures inside them. These inside figures are respectively black, white, and cross-hatched. The missing drawing is made up by noting which of these features do not occur in the other two figures in that row.)

31. 22. (Multiply the number in the first column by that in the second column, and subtract from the product the number in the second column. 2 × 12 = 24; 24 − 2 = 22.)

32. ACHE. (Take the letters corresponding to the numbers (i.e. A = 1, B = 2, etc.) in reverse order.)

33. Playpen. (All the others have four feet.)

34. 4. (Multiply the numbers to the right and left of the triangle, and divide by the number underneath. 8 × 12 = 96; $\frac{96}{24} = 4$.)

35. x. (Each letter in the third column is twice the number of letters removed from the letter in the second column, as is each letter in the second column from the corresponding letter in the first column. There are two letters between P and s, and four letters between s and x.)

36. 78. (All the other numbers are squares.)

37. z. (The bottom letter is four, six, eight, and finally ten places in the alphabet removed from the top letter; the tenth letter after P is z.)

38. 67. (Double each number and add successively one, two, three, etc. 2 × 32 = 64 + 3 = 67.)

39. Christopher Columbus. (Write the numbers from 0 to 9 over the first ten letters of the alphabet; the numbers corresponding to BAGG are 1066, associated with William the Conqueror. The numbers corresponding to BEJC are 1492, the year Columbus discovered America.)

40. 1152. (Multiply the figure at the bottom by the square of the number at the left; divide by the number on the right.)

Test Seven

1. F. (Each successive letter jumps two places backwards in the alphabet.)

2. Socrates. (The others are composers.)

3. 16. (Numbers proceed by alternate steps of + 2, − 3, + 4, − 5. 19 − 3 = 16.)

4. Madrid. (Each of the others lies approximately 10 degrees of latitude farther south than the preceding one.)

5. Moose. (The moose is larger than the leopard, the horse, the skunk, the tiger, the zebra, and the rabbit.)

6. PER.

7. 5. (The black area rotates ninety degrees each time.)

8. Hit. (The word in the middle has the same meaning as the two words at either side; to strike is to hit, and a hit is a success.)

9. 4. (Spirals are either once round, one and a half times round, or half a time round, an example of each occurring only once in any one line or column.)

10. 39. (Each number is twice the preceding one, with one, two, three, four, etc., subtracted. Thus 2 × 22 − 5 = 39.)

11.   5 and 6. (The star is rotating through one position to the right (clockwise) each time, the cross and circle rotate through one position counter-clockwise each time. 5 and 6, if their positions were interchanged, would continue this sequence.)

12.   x. (The letters in this series are the third letters after each of the five vowels; x is the third letter after u.)

13.   256. (The numbers at the top of each domino are doubled each time, those at the bottom are squared; the square of 16 is 256.)

14.   RIP, ONE, ALE, *or* ILL.

15.   Bow. (As golf-ball and ball-game go together, so do rainbow and bowsprit.)

16.   5. (Each number in the bottom row is the sum of the numbers in the first and second rows, minus one. 5 + 1 − 1 = 5.)

17.   1. (In each row and column there are two, three, or four wheels; a black, white, or shaded front; a long, short, or medium funnel; and one, two, or three stripes. The cabin has one, two, or no windows. This determines what the missing locomotive looks like.)

18.   33. (The figures in the centre row are made up by adding the figure in the first row to twice the figure in the last row. 13 + 20 = 33.)

19.   Slip. (All these words can be prefixed by 'land'.)

20.   AGO.

21.   Skiing. (Rugby, football, and polo are team sports.)

22. 26. (Add the numbers at the top and bottom and then subtract the numbers at right and left.)

23. 2. (The second figure is the only one which has no parts enclosed by either curved or straight lines.)

24. PORT. (The word in brackets is made up of the second and first letters of the words outside the brackets, in that order.)

25. Swell. (A swell is a smart person, and to swell is to bulge.)

26. 3. (It contains curved lines; none of the others do.)

27. APE.

28.

15
O

(Numbers go up by four each time, and the letter in each case is the 3rd, 7th, 11th, and 15th in the alphabet.)

29. 662. (The number in the brackets is formed by adding the two numbers outside the brackets and doubling. 214 + 117 = 331 × 2 = 662.)

30. NIGHT.

31. 4. (The figure in the square can be a triangle, a semi-circle, or a wave, and it can be either white, black, or shaded. The circle at the top can be right, left, or centre, and the three arrows can be distributed in three ways. The missing figure must therefore be a shaded semi-circle, with the circle in the left corner and one arrow to the right and two to the left.)

32. 197. (All the others are squares, 197 is not.)

33. 24. (Subtract the sum of the numbers in the first two columns from their product. $(6 \times 6) - (6 + 6) = 24$.) *Or* 18. (First number plus twice second number.)

34. Unicorn. (In all the other words the first and last vowels are identical.)

35. 23. (Double the preceding number and subtract two, three, four, etc. $2 \times 14 = 28 - 5 = 23$.) *Or* 22. (Add the two preceding numbers and subtract 1.)

36. x. (These are two series, starting with c and o respectively; in each, two letters are skipped to give the next letter. Two letters skipped from u gives x.)

37. ANT.

38. 39. (Numbers alternately increase by five and decrease by two.)

39. 25. (Each threesome is made up by taking one of the numbers, squaring it, and dividing by two; the other two, multiplied together, then give this number. Thus half of $32^2 = 512$, which is 16×32. Half of $48^2 = 1152$, which is 8×144. Half of $40^2 = 800$, which is 32×25, hence the missing number is 25.)

40. g; the number 2 is also a permissible answer. (The corresponding letters and numbers are:
A B C D E F G H I J
4 6 9 1 5 8 2 7 0 3)

Test Eight

1. g. (Letters jump three places backwards in the alphabet.)

2. August. (It has no 'r' in it.)

3. 21. (Each figure is half the preceding one, plus ten. Half of 22 = 11 + 10 = 21.)

4. Denmark. (Denmark is the only kingdom among these countries.)

5. Sleigh. (Unlike the cart, the truck, the bicycle, and the carriage, the sleigh has no wheels.)

6. Grouse. (A grouse is a fowl, and to grouse is to grumble.)

7. GAIN.

8. 2. (The black line rotates clockwise through 90 degrees at each turn.)

9. 6. (The figures in the third row are made up from the large part of the figure in the second row and the small part of the figure in the first row; shading alternates from row to row.)

10. 35. (Going clockwise, each number is the preceding one, multiplied by two, and with three subtracted. 19 × 2 = 38 − 3 = 35.)

11. 4. (1 and 5, and 2 and 3, are pairs; they are rotated through 180 degrees relative to each other, and black and white are interchanged. 4 does not fit into this scheme.)

12. L. (The letters in the second column are three, two, and four letters forward in the alphabet from those in the first column; those in the third column are three times as many letters backward in the alphabet, i.e. nine, six, and twelve letters removed. Twelve letters back from x is L.)

13. 47. (Halve the number at the top, and add the number at the bottom.)

14. INK.

15. Table and stable. (S + table = stable.)

16. 4. (Take the square of the difference between the first two numbers to make the third. $6 - 4 = 2$; $2^2 = 4$.) *Or* 8. Difference between columns 1 and 2, multiplied by 2, 3, and 4.)

17. 1. (There are three kinds of body, which can be white, black, or shaded; three kinds of neck, which can be straight, curved, or kinky; three types of head, either round, square, or triangular; and three kinds of tail – up, down, or straight. Each of these features occurs only once in each row or column, and this determines the combination of features in the missing dragon.)

18. Lily. (All these words can be prefixed by the word 'water'.)

19. PEST.

20. Madrid. (The others are Pisa, Milan, and Florence.)

21. 35. (Multiply the three numbers outside the triangle, and divide by two.)

22. 3. (Drawing number 3 contains more than four enclosed spaces.)

23. 219. (The number in the brackets is three times the difference between the numbers outside the brackets.)

24. Stake. (A stick is a stake, and a stake is a wager.)

25. 1. (The minute hand goes back in five-minute steps, the hour hand goes forward by two-hour steps.)

26. B. (The letters in the three rows, read backwards, spell out the words gird, dirt, and bird.)

27.

P
K

(The letters at the top are formed by taking the fourth letter following the preceding one, those at the bottom by doing the same, but going backwards in the alphabet. The fourth letter from L is P; the fourth letter from O, going backwards, is K.)

28. Tote. (The word in the brackets is made up of the two letters preceding the last letter in the words on either side of the brackets.)

29. GENT.

30. 381. (All these numbers are divisible by three.)

31. 27. (Multiply the top and bottom numbers, and divide by four.)

32. 15. (There are two sequences of numbers, alternating with each other. Both go up by two, then by three, then by four, etc. 11 + 4 = 15.)

33. 2. (In each row one of the rings is white, one is cross-hatched, one is black; one triangle in the middle is white, one is cross-hatched, one is black; the line sticking out of the triangle is affixed to each side in turn; the two figures outside the ring assume one of three positions. Combining these requirements gives the correct solution.)

34. Pit. (All these words can be used to prefix the word 'fall'; only 'pit' can be so used of the words in the second line.)

35. 408. (The number in the brackets is twice the difference between the numbers before and after the brackets; 648 − 444 = 204; 2 × 204 = 408.)

36. 9. (Nine is not a prime number; it is divisible by three.)

37. ARE.

38. 36. (Numbers are alternately multiplied by three and divided by two. $12 \times 3 = 36$.)

39. UDLOTWIN. (High is to low as up is to down. The letters of these words are alternated with nonsense letters in the above words.)

40. 29. (Alternate numbers form two series. The one beginning with 260 requires four to be subtracted, and the resulting number to be divided by two. $62 - 4 = 58$, and $\dfrac{58}{2} = 29$. The other series is formed by halving the preceding figure.)

Transforming Scores into I.Q.s

To find your I.Q., enter your score on the baseline of the appropriate graph on the next two pages. Draw a line straight up until it meets the diagonal line. The point on the vertical line corresponding to this gives your I.Q. As an example, in the first graph a score of ten points = I.Q.100 is illustrated. The scores are accurate within the following limits:

TEST	SCORE
1, 2	10–22
3, 4	9–21
5, 7, 8	7–19
6	11–23

Beyond these limits too much reliance should not be placed upon them.

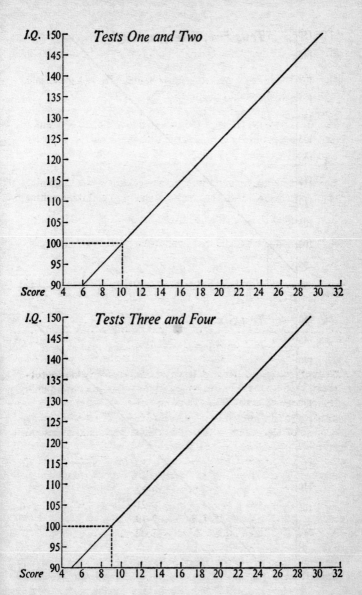

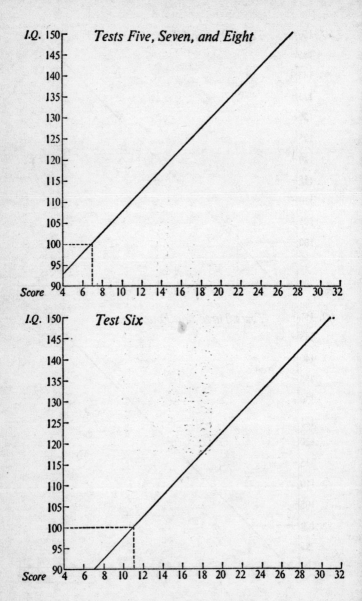

Tests Five, Seven, and Eight

Test Six